OECD
PROGRAMME ON EDUCATIONAL BUILDING

PROVIDING FOR FUTURE CHANGE

ADAPTABILITY AND FLEXIBILITY IN SCHOOL BUILDING

ORGANISATION FOR ECONOMIC CO-OPERATION AND DEVELOPMENT

The Organisation for Economic Co-operation and Development (OECD) was set up under a Convention signed in Paris on 14th December, 1960, which provides that the OECD shall promote policies designed:
- to achieve the highest sustainable economic growth and employment and a rising standard of living in Member countries, while maintaining financial stability, and thus to contribute to the development of the world economy;
- to contribute to sound economic expansion in Member as well as non-member countries in the process of economic development;
- to contribute to the expansion of world trade on a multilateral, non-discriminatory basis in accordance with international obligations.

The Members of OECD are Australia, Austria, Belgium, Canada, Denmark, Finland, France, the Federal Republic of Germany, Greece, Iceland, Ireland, Italy, Japan, Luxembourg, the Netherlands, New Zealand, Norway, Portugal, Spain, Sweden, Switzerland, Turkey, the United Kingdom and the United States.

The Programme on Educational Building (PEB) was established by the Council of the Organisation for Economic Co-operation and Development as from January 1972. Its present mandate expires at the end of 1976.

The main objectives of the Programme are:
- *to facilitate the exchange of information and experience on aspects of educational building judged to be important by participating Member countries;*
- *to promote co-operation between such Member countries regarding the technical bases for improving the quality, speed and cost effectiveness of school construction.*

The Programme functions within the Directorate for Social Affairs, Manpower and Education of the Organisation in accordance with the decisions of the Council of the Organisation, under the authority of the Secretary-General. It is directed by a Steering Committee of senior government officials, and financed by participating governments.

* * *

© OECD, 1976.
Queries concerning permissions or translation rights should be addressed to:
Director of Information, OECD
2, rue André-Pascal, 75775 PARIS CEDEX 16, France.

CONTENTS

PREFACE

Part One
GENERAL PURPOSE OF THE STUDY

Objectives	9
Definitions	9
Method of Work	10
Case Examples	12
Layout of the Report	12

Part Two
CASE STUDIES

The Purpose of the Case Studies	15

CASE STUDY IN FLEXIBILITY: MAIDEN ERLEGH 15

As Existing	16
As a Junior School	18
As a Non-vocational Adult Education Centre	20
As a Unit more Intensively Used	22
As a Department of Modern Studies (Upper School)	24
As a Science and Mathematics Centre (Upper School)	26

CASE STUDIES IN ADAPTABILITY

Bases for the Sucy-en-Brie and Arlington Exercises	28

THE ENGLISH MODEL

Broad Objectives. Social and Curriculum Organisation	29
Design Decisions or Assumptions	35

SUCY-EN-BRIE

The School as Existing	35
Fitting the Model into the Building	40
Adjustments to the Model	41
Summary of Modifications to the English Model	44
The Solution	47
Degrees of Adaptability	56

ARLINGTON
  The School as Existing 58
  Fitting the Model into the Building 58
  Summary of Modifications to the English Model 68
  The Solution 71
  Degrees of Adaptability 78

Part Three
IMPLICATIONS OF PROVIDING FOR CHANGE
  Institutional and Managerial Arrangements 81
  Space Sub-Division and Layout 84
  Plan Form and Building Envelope 89
  Location and Siting 93
  Environment and Services 96
  Structure 98
  Furniture and Equipment 100
  Cost Considerations 102

Part Four
SUMMARY OF CONCLUSIONS
  Education 107
  Management 107
  Finance and Planning 108
  Technology 108
  Design 108

AKNOWLEDGEMENTS 109

PREFACE

The initial studies undertaken within the framework of the OECD Programme on Educational Building have all shown that getting value for money in school building is determined by the extent to which the buildings can be made to match educational requirements.

The present report, which is the fourth in a series published under the Programme, represents an extension of this earlier work in so far as it raises a new set of problems: the educational requirements which school buildings have to meet evolve rapidly and unless the buildings can be made to accommodate future change, they are liable to early and costly obsolescence.

Many of the changes which the buildings should allow for are only in part foreseeable. Nonetheless, it is possible to distinguish between two major types of changes: those linked to the evolution of the demand for education either because the numbers to be accommodated vary over time or because the needs concern new age groups or categories of the population; and those linked to the evolution of teaching/learning practices and activities. The latter type of changes are more complex than it may at first appear, since the educational methods now gaining currency are increasingly characterized by the frequency of change in the nature, balance, sequence and interrelations of activities.

An important contribution of the present study is the distinction it makes between adaptability and flexibility. Adaptability has been defined as the quality of a building which enables subsequent alteration to be made to its physical fabric, i.e. facilitates adaptation—essentially large magnitude/low frequency change. Flexibility on the other hand is the quality of a building which permits variation in activities without the need for adaptation—essentially low magnitude/high frequency change.

Another interesting feature of this study is the method of work adopted. Based, as all the studies of the Programme, on real examples drawn from a number of countries, the method consisted in subjecting each of the cases selected to a unique theoretical exercise. To anticipate future change, a series of conceivable alternatives were defined in relation to which the problems likely to emerge in providing for such change were studied. The first exercise consisted in examining to what extent a given building could accommodate a different range of activities or different educational functions than those for which it had originally been planned. The second type of exercise consisted in testing under what conditions an existing school building could be adapted to an entirely different educational model than that for which it had originally been designed. In addition to enabling the hypotheses of the study to be tested against the background of reality, the method also offers the advantage of suggesting an approach which designers and educationists in different countries might profitably apply in their own work.

It is hoped, therefore, that the present report will prove useful not only to policy-makers anxious to provide buildings which will remain fully efficient throughout their life-span but also to designers, often more responsive than others to the realities of change, who are seeking new solutions to the problem of providing for future change. Finally, the report also indicates to teachers how they can make better use of the potential for change offered by buildings or the way in which they can contribute to the design of new schools so that the working environment provided will be both more flexible and adaptable than in the past.

The report is published under the responsibility of the Secretariat which wishes to record its appreciation to all those who have contributed to the study, in particular: Mr Paul Lenssen, architect-consultant, who acted as the rapporteur; Mr Desmond Williams and his collaborators, especially Miss Kathy Johnson-Marshall, who carried out all the architectural studies; Mr Eric Pearson, formerly member of Her Britannic Majesty's Inspectorate who defined and formulated the conceivable alternatives and the educational model used; and Professor Guy Oddie, senior adviser to the Programme, for his contribution in drawing the main conclusions of the study.

Part one
GENERAL PURPOSE OF THE STUDY

Objectives

1. In a great many countries there is increasing interest in the need for school buildings to be able to cope in some measure with change in educational requirements. The interest arises first from a recognition that educational methods can be subjected to rapid and frequent change, so that schools built to meet contemporary methods may well be liable to early obsolescence. Second is the assumption that the size of teaching spaces may need frequent and rapid alteration to fit variations in size of teaching group consequent on a wider range of pupil choice between alternative courses. And, thirdly, some architects believe that for the best match between environment and education teacher control over room shape, size and so on should be maximised.

2. How far each of these views is justifiable is a matter which this study sets out to examine. A number of developments has occurred giving practical examples of widely differing approaches to the problem of providing for change. Some have sought to provide complete adaptability in terms of relocatable partitions (that is to say, partitions which can be more easily demounted and repositioned at will) illumination and services; others have adopted less thorough but, at the same time, less costly approaches. The objective of the study is to bring together experience representative of these recent international developments and clarify its architectural, educational and financial implications.

Definitions

3. First consideration of this topic immediately gives rise to a number of major questions concerning:

i) the kind of educational and other changes which, if and when they occur, will affect school buildings; and
ii) the frequency and magnitude of such changes.

4. Certain kinds of change may necessitate extension or change to the fabric and services of the original building—in short, adaptation. Thus, following from the above questions emerge further questions regarding:

i) the elements or components of school building which will need to be adaptable to accommodate changes and the possibilities of relocation, replacement, removal or addition they offer;
ii) the constraints on the relocation, replacement, etc., of these elements or components imposed by other elements—for example, by staircases which for all practical purposes can be considered as non-relocatable—and how such constraints can be minimised;
iii) the relationship between ease of adaptation and plan form;
iv) the direct and indirect cost, if any, involved in providing adaptable buildings and in subsequent adaptation when it occurs;
v) the managerial problems raised both by

such initial provision and then by its subsequent use when the need arises.

5. Yet this further set of questions deals with one way only of coping with the problems set by changes in the use of buildings—namely, by making them adaptable. Everyday experience shows that there are other ways; a cursory look at the question of "frequency and magnitude of changes" suggests that change can be considered as falling into two broad categories: large magnitude/low frequency change and low magnitude/high frequency change. Bearing in mind that the adaptation of buildings hardly constitutes a first aim in itself and the key issue is how different kinds of change can best be provided for with regard to time, effort and financial constraints, two quite distinct concepts emerge and can be expressed as follows:

— adaptability, the quality of a building which facilitates adaptation; adaptation may require relocation, replacement, removal or addition in respect of either the constructional elements, services or the finishes of the building—essentially large magnitude/low frequency change; and
— flexibility, the quality of a building which permits variation in the activities, timetabling, class size, etc., of a school without the need for adaptation as defined—essentially low magnitude/high frequency change.

6. These two qualities are not necessarily mutually exclusive in any one building—indeed, providing for change may well involve both in order to be successful. But each has architectural, educational and financial implications which are particular and which require particular clarification. Arising out of the concept of flexibility therefore, are further major questions akin to those outlined above concerning adaptability [paragraph 4 i) to v)]. These concern:

  i) the elements, components, attributes of school buildings which have an important bearing on the accommodation of educational or other changes while, at the same time, not in themselves being adaptable in the sense already defined;
  ii) the possibilities of permitting greater variation in the activity patterns permitted or facilitated by such elements, components or attributes;
  iii) the inherent constraints or limitations on this variation and how they can be minimised;
  iv) the cost implications of flexibility;
  v) the managerial problems raised by flexibility.

Method of Work

7. Plainly no definitive answers can be given to the first questions posed above concerning the kind of educational or other changes which will take place, their frequency and magnitude [paragraph 3 *i)* and *ii)*]. But the sort of changes which may possibly occur might be categorised as follows:

Change in type and/or level of education. Whether such change results from structural reform of the educational system or from demographic changes or from changes in urban patterns is immaterial to this study. This kind of change might involve alteration in the number of people to be accommodated and therefore change in the number of workplaces provided. For example, on space standards alone, a building designed for a certain number of infants would be re-designed for half or even one third of the same number of further education students. These are extremes but they illustrate the point. Even space standards for primary and secondary schools are in the ratio of 4 : 7 as far as England is concerned. Thus the significant changes would be: changes in the numbers to be accommodated; changes in the range and nature of activities to be pursued; and changes in the relative numbers pursuing such activities.

Change in the balance of activities. With fixed numbers in a school where all pupils follow the same curriculum and programme, the maximum number engaged in any activity at one time can be closely estimated. Where there are options however, the numbers choosing each option will vary periodically and so will the numbers engaged on each activity. An excess of workplaces or facility to change their function is essential to the operation of optional courses.

Change in the inter-relation of activities. Change of this nature is often consequent on the breaking down of subject barriers. An example is the teaching in England of subjects like drawing and painting, wood and metalwork, dress-making, domestic science. At one time each was treated entirely separately from the rest, woodwork and metalwork being exclusively for the boys and dress-making and domestic science for the girls. Eventually it was realised that boys and girls were equally interested in all these subjects and that each could contribute to the other. So in new schools facilities for these subjects are now closely related to each other whereas formerly they were separate. Such change in fact goes much further than this: it involves not only reconsideration of the respective interests of boys and girls but also of the relationship between theory and practice and of the emphasis given to various aspects of activities undertaken. For instance, dress-making becomes fashion and design, domestic science becomes home economics and covers a much broader field of human interest. Aspects of science are sometimes related to social studies and accommodation for physical education, dance, drama and music are related to provide integrated courses in the performing arts.

Change in activity sequence. One example of such change follows from the reconsideration of the relationship between theory and practice just mentioned where, for instance, the mode of teaching in which one hour of theory is followed by two hours of practical class changes to a mode where theory and practice are interwoven as the need arises and where the same facility is used for both. At one time "The Library" in a secondary school was a secluded facility used for private individual study at set periods—very different from the modern concept of resource-based activities in which the many and varied resources for learning may be arranged at a number of points in relation to the learning facilities. The sequence of activities is then subject to considerable variation, sometimes dictated by the student alone.

Change in group organisation and mode of learning. From many possible examples two may serve. One is the change from uniform classes of about 30 pupils each to groups varying from a few pupils (possibly working on their own) to regular and frequent audiences of 100 or so in a briefing session. Another is the increased emphasis on discovery and experiment—on active as opposed to passive learning. Such a mode involves a school in providing effective learning experience for the pupils.

Introduction of new activities. This may result either from a change in the mode of learning or from the increased range of information and communication media becoming available. Examples abound of new activities which have had to be fitted into schools: collecting data locally to establish the course of urban changes; a study of retail shopping to establish the course of inflation; helping the aged and the handicapped; building and using computers.

Technological innovation. Sometimes activities or modes of learning may remain unchanged but nevertheless some technological innovation calls for change in the building or its use. An example is the substitution of computers for card-index systems as a means of reference.

Non-educational change. Change of a non-educational origin may nonetheless have to be coped with. Such change may stem from pressures to secure more effective use of under-used accommodation, or from a rise in standards affecting lighting, heating, fire protection, means of escape, etc. Some change may stem entirely from social pressures; for example, the provision of meals, keeping children off the streets in the evenings and during holidays (schools often become "play-centres" at such times), youth centres which function as nurseries during the day. Under this head can be included changes in the financial resources available for educational development; for example, difficulties in meeting teaching area requirements in times of inflation and recession, cut-backs in the supply of books, materials and equipment—these call for initiative and resource on the part of teachers in doing more with less and may also make different demands of the school building.

Foreseeable change. The foregoing types of change will usually be such that they cannot be foreseen when a building is first conceived. But it can be the case that change is of a kind which can be foreseen and for which the original concept can allow. Such a case arises when demographic change can be forecast so that, for instance, the number of pupils attending the school will rise after a period, and then after reaching a peak will again fall off.

Changes in the supply of teachers. Changes in this field can affect teacher-pupil ratios and have significant implications for the building. When ratios are generous, more tutoring and small group work is possible. A shortage of science teachers may result in "chalk and talk" types of teaching rather than experimentation by the pupils; or a shortage of fully-qualified art teachers might be met by the employment of unqualified personnel to support the qualified teachers; this in turn would lead to a need for greater supervision and contact and an arrangement of teaching space to allow this.

8. It is changes of this kind that, singly or in combination may occur. Apart from foreseeable or planned changes, there is an inevitable uncertainty about the future; nevertheless, it can be to some extent anticipated as a series of conceivable alternatives in relation to which practical judgment can be exercised in making policy choices.

9. It was in relation to these conceivable alternatives that the study was carried out.

A number of real examples was taken of school buildings each of which had been conceived to serve the needs of a particular educational model. The question was then asked: what adaptation would be needed if each building had to be adapted to serve a different educational model—a conceivable alternative to the original one? Thus the implications of change for school buildings, their elements, components, attributes, plan form, etc., were experienced and demonstrated in a practical way and from this experience inferences were drawn concerning the questions posed above [paragraph 4 i) to v), paragraph 6 i) to v)].

Case Examples

10. The selection of case examples aimed at giving a broad coverage of the range of problems likely to be encountered in providing for change. These problems differ from case to case according to the original provision made: the nature and degree of provision vary—the Lower School Block of Maiden Erlegh School, Berkshire, England, largely relies on the approach embodied in the concept of flexibility; the Collège d'enseignement secondaire (C.E.S.), Sucy-en-Brie, France, demonstrates an attempt to provide adaptability but within strictly defined economic limits; and Arlington Senior High School, Ontario, Canada, goes even further along the path of provision of adaptability, the building system in which it is built probably representing the most thorough attempt to achieve complete adaptability to be found anywhere.

11. The "conceivable alternatives" referred to above (paragraph 9) likewise differed in an attempt to demonstrate the effect of a range of different types or degrees of change. In the Maiden Erlegh exercise the changes of use are the kinds which could occur in reality: they do not represent an attempt to imagine some radically new form of education (which would, in any case, be of questionable value) but are simply the changes which would arise if a different kind of already existing activity had to be accommodated. In the other exercises, the Sucy-en-Brie C.E.S. and Arlington Senior High School are subjected to much more radical change: into these school buildings are put schools of comparable size to the ones currently housed as regards numbers but based on an entirely different pedagogical alternative inherent in which are various assumptions concerning "the kind of educational and other changes which... will affect school buildings..." (paragraph 3). The changes include: change in type of education; the introduction of new activities; changes in the balance of activities, their inter-relation and sequence; changes in mode of learning; and non-educational change arising from different norms governing the different standards to be observed.

12. It must be emphasised beyond any possibility of misunderstanding that the pedagogical alternative adopted does not represent the slightest suggestion that the education at present provided in the case examples selected will ultimately follow the alternative patterns. The intention in each case is simply to explore the problems of adaptation which arise in accommodating a particular educational model in a building conceived for a very different model. Because the models, particularly in the Sucy-en-Brie exercise, differ so radically, this comes as near to representing the unforeseeable as can be imagined. In this way these exercises go further towards simulating the unforeseeable than the Maiden Erlegh one which attempts solely to accommodate changes of a known kind which could occur with, say, certain demographic changes.

Layout of the Report

13. The report is laid out in a form which, it is hoped, will enable different readers—administrators, policy-makers, teachers, designers—to extract what interests them in particular. Thus, immediately following this presentation of the general purpose of the study, Part Two details all the work carried out on the case examples outlined in paragraphs 10 to 12. Part Three then sets out the arguments and findings which lead to the conclusions of this study; it discusses the implications of providing for future change: first, the implications for institutional and managerial arrangements—primarily aimed at policy-makers and administrators; and second, the implications for the various physical characteristics of the school building (space subdivision and layout, plan form and building envelope, location and siting, environment and services, structure, furniture and equipment)—more technical in nature than the previous and, though perhaps of interest to policy-makers and administrators, aimed more at designers and day-to-day users (directors, teachers, inspectors). A section on the cost considerations involved in the provision of flexibility and/or adaptability concludes Part Three; and a summary of major conclusions, directed at a general readership, makes up Part Four.

Part two
CASE STUDIES

The Purpose of the Studies

14. The principles established and the conclusions reached in Part Three of this report are not solely the outcome of logical argument. The lines of argument emerged through probings into the qualities of flexibility and adaptability evident in the school buildings of many Member countries. It became clear however that their validity needed to be tested in much deeper case studies in order to lend authority to the arguments. The evidence on which the arguments are based is presented in considerable detail in the cases which follow, so that the assumptions made might be understood and questioned where necessary, and alternative conclusions advanced. Three cases were selected to provide a broad coverage of the problems likely to be encountered; firstly, in meeting short-term evolutionary change in educational methods or in local services; and secondly, in providing for major, radical change to meet the demands of entirely different educational modes and objectives. Hence:

i) The Maiden Erlegh exercise explores the possibility of variation of educational activity and function within a building without the need for major physical change, namely, the quality of flexibility. These are changes in the use of a building which a school may make for itself e.g. in the functions or workings of a department, or which an education authority may find it necessary to make in the re-organisation of local education services. They are such as could occur in reality within the foreseeable future.

ii) In the Sucy-en-Brie (France) and Arlington (Canada) exercises, the schools have been subjected to a radical change of educational mode from that for which the schools were originally planned, necessitating substantial physical change to the buildings. The contrasting plan forms of the two schools raise equally contrasting problems of their adaptation to the English model and serve to explore the limits of adaptability on a broader front than would otherwise be the case. The English model chosen should not be seen as one likely to develop in the countries concerned, but only as a "conceivable alternative" (see paragraphs 8, 9 and 11) to the modes operating in the two schools at the present time. It was devised only to test the qualities of adaptability inherent in the buildings.

15. For each case example a short description is set out of the building (including plans as existing) and of how far adaptability and/or flexibility were originally envisaged. This is followed in the case of Maiden Erlegh with a short description of the changes of use to which the building was subjected and plans showing how these changes could be accommodated—some without and some with a degree of physical alteration. In the more elaborate exercises—on Sucy-en-Brie and Arlington—the description of the buildings as existing and their plans is preceded by an outline of the common hypothetical pedagogical model which formed the basis for both works of adaptation and of the key decisions or assumptions made governing the work undertaken and concerning, for example, norms, design guidelines and standards of provision common to both exercises. There follows, in each case, a commentary on the work, the problems encountered and the reasons for the numerous decisions taken which led to the new proposals to accommodate this model. These proposals are described in the form of plans and short texts covering aspects which do not lend themselves to graphical representation; finally, area analyses of the buildings, before and after adaptation, are given.

CASE STUDY IN FLEXIBILITY : MAIDEN ERLEGH

16. The following six plans illustrate the flexibility in use and adaptability to future change of the Lower School Unit at the Maiden Erlegh Secondary School, Berkshire, England. Plan 1 illustrates the form and layout of the building as it is at present used. Plans 2, 3 and 4 show changes of function effected solely by the relocation of furniture, movable storage units and screens. Plans 5 and 6 involve some removal and relocation of internal walls, but on a very modest scale, and Plan 6 also requires an extension of existing services (electricity, gas, water, drainage). Any physical changes to the building would be of a minor character. In all these examples, the unit retains its administrative offices for the use of departmental staff, and can thus retain a considerable degree of autonomy. The quiet, carpeted central areas of the unit provide focal points for the development of social life.

Plan 1 : AS EXISTING (Lower Scho

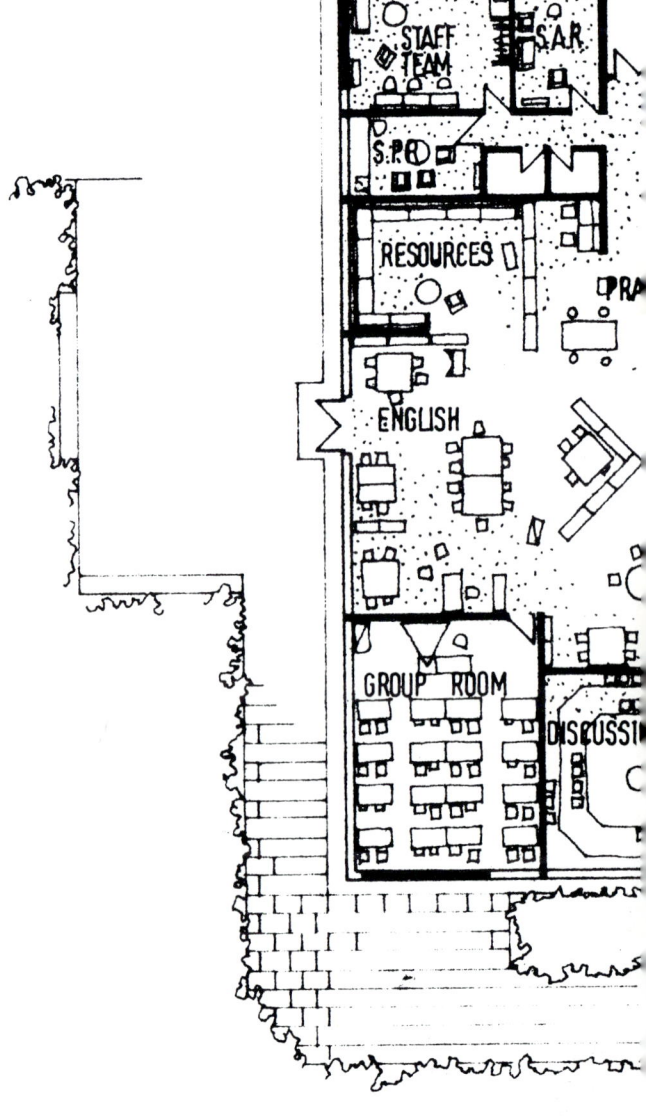

While the unit has been designed to serve as a base for 480 boys and girls aged 11 to 13 years, it takes an average teaching load of 240. The open design is broken up by a number of closed spaces. These give a sense of containment to working groups in the open areas and help to provide physical zones for curriculum development. A large, closed central teaching space, well-insulated from the rest of the teaching accommodation, is used for drama, music, dancing and for lectures to large groups. Three other closed spaces provide for conventional teaching to classes of about 30 and there is a tiered discussion space for up to 40 pupils. The science laboratory, with peripheral services, is very flexible in use and opens on to a general area given over to mathematics. The extensive open teaching area, carpeted throughout to reduce noise interference, is capable of considerable variation in use. It is articulated by movable open-shelf and wardrobe units, and can be arranged for a great variety of activities whether of a bookish or practical nature. A carpeted social area adjoins the central drama space. The work done in the unit covers 50 to 60 per cent of the Lower School curriculum. It is planned to encourage individual learning within a wide choice of educational opportunities.

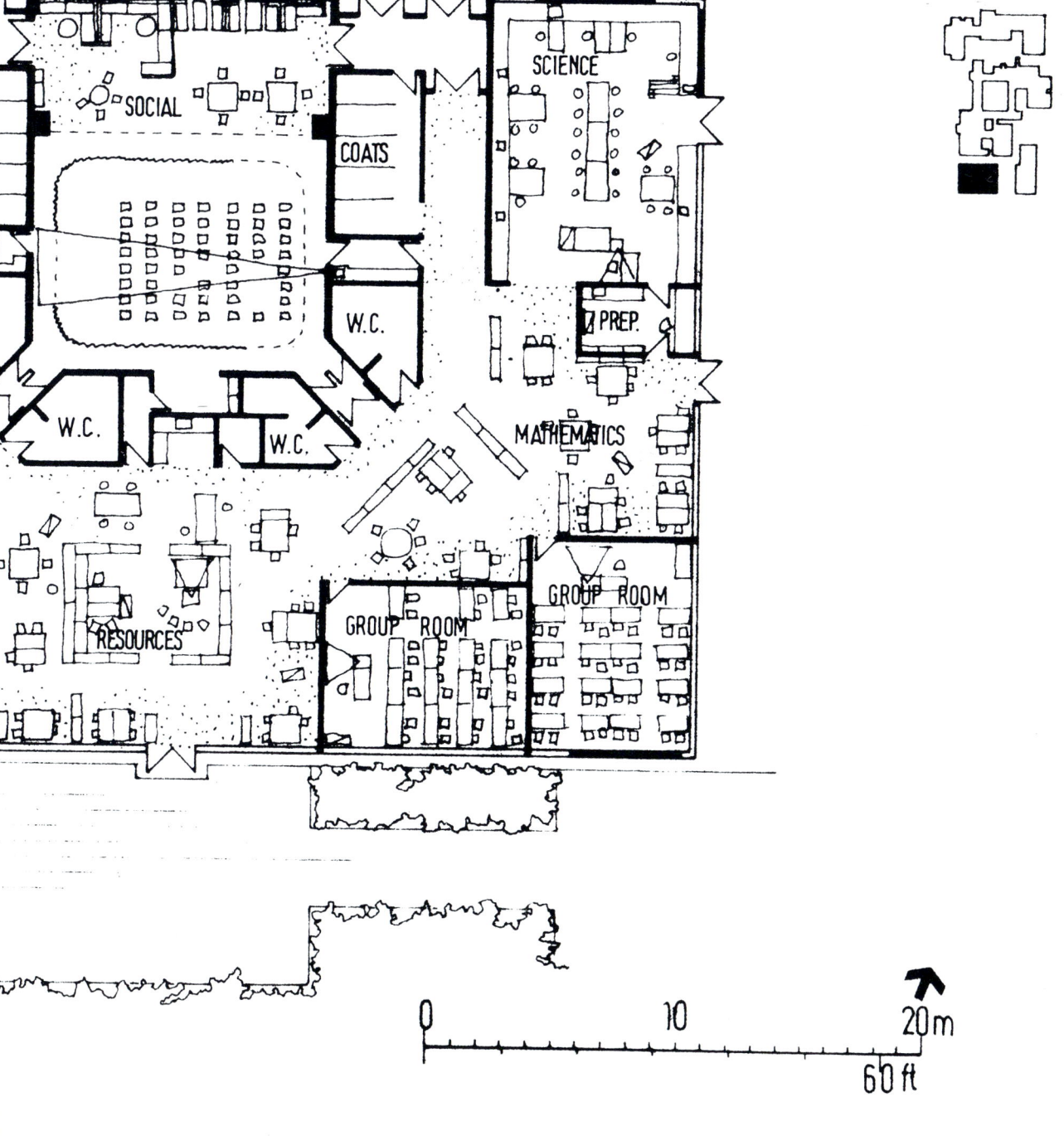

Plan 2 : AS A JUNIOR SCHOOL

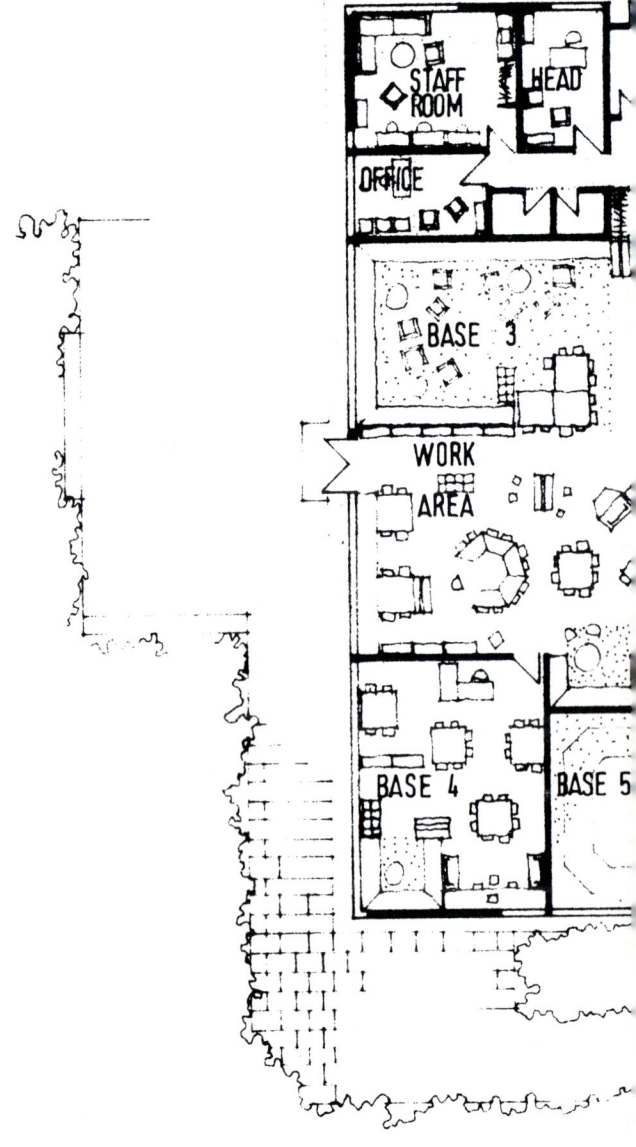

The layout shows how the unit could serve for a Junior School of 320 boys and girls aged 8 to 11 years. A Local Education Authority may find itself temporarily short of primary school places, but with an excess of secondary school places. Alternatively, a junior school may at some future date fall into a new institutional pattern, at present unforeseen. There are bases for eight classes, some of which are in closed spaces, as well as extensive open areas for project and investigation work. The latter is supported by a library and resources area. The largest base is given over to elementary science and practical mathematics and part of the adjoining open area is assigned to arts and crafts. The central drama/music space is retained. Thus there are many opportunities to vary the activities and develop a wide-ranging work programme. The accommodation provides for the whole junior school curriculum other than physical education for which provision would need to be made elsewhere. These facilities already exist on the site and could no doubt be made available.

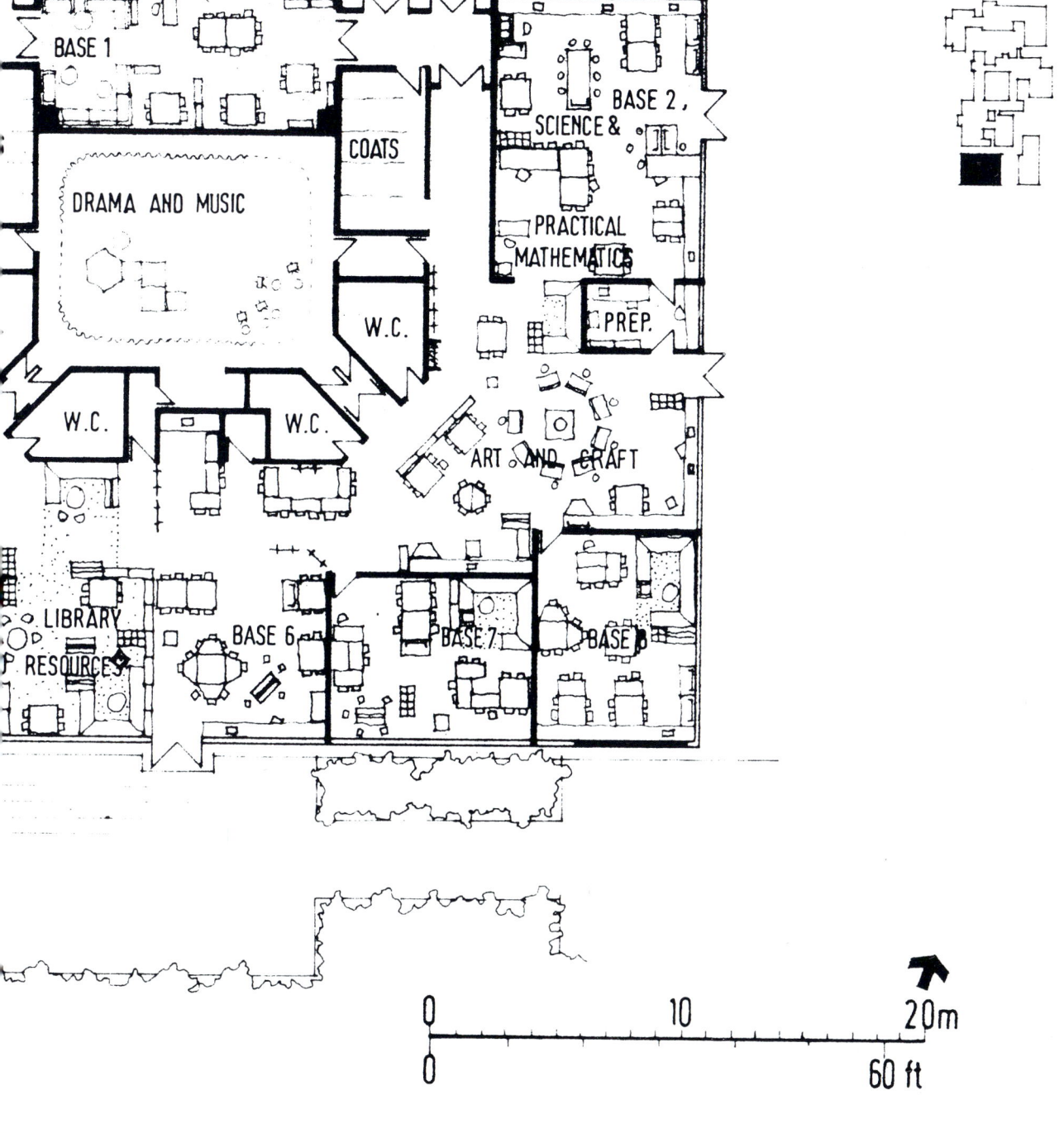

Plan 3 : AS A NON-VOCATION

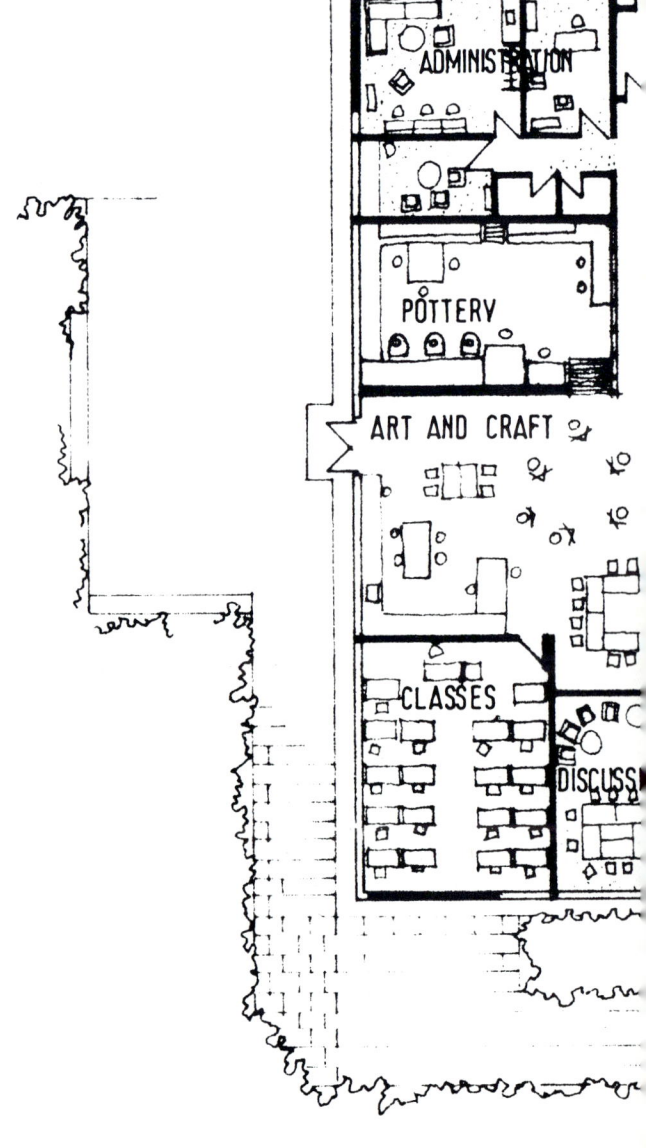

Modified institutional arrangements might lead to the establishment of a centre for adult studies and interests, operating in both day and evening and probably at the weekends. The closed, central space is used for lectures and meetings and by drama and music groups. There are five closed spaces; the largest is for science and mathematics; another adjoins a unit-kitchen area and is for lectures and demonstrations in home economics and for the use of needlework and dress-design groups; three further spaces are for class and discussion groups in philosophy, languages and humanities. The open areas can be varied in their functions. The plan shows a large library and informal reading area with adjoining snack-bar facilities, flanked on one side by a large painting, pottery and craft area, and on the other, by a cooking and general home-making space. A workshop is situated behind the central drama space. The unit could work as an autonomous institution if need be and provide a variety of courses. Adults interested in physical education or sport, or requiring highly technical courses, would be catered for elsewhere.

ADULT EDUCATION CENTRE

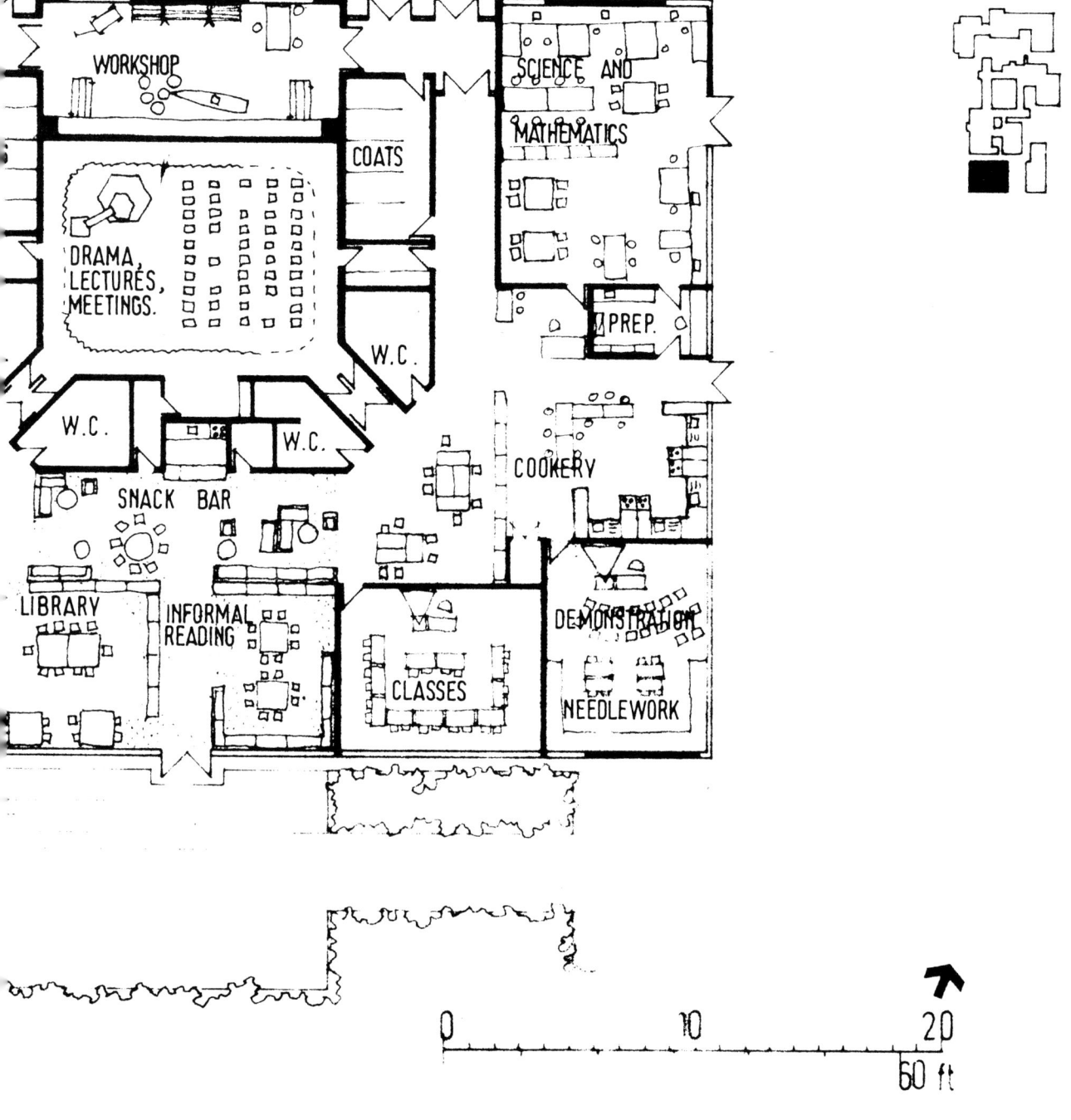

Plan 4: AS A UNIT MO[RE INTENSIVELY USED]

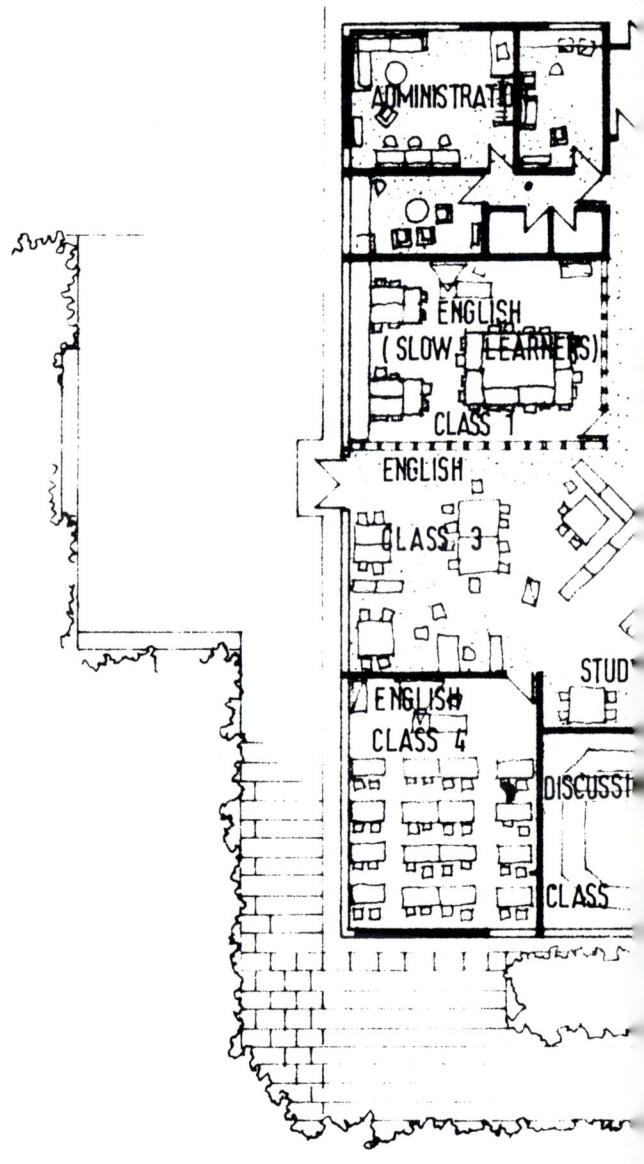

A school frequently works under pressure of numbers in excess of those for which it was originally designed, especially in areas of rapid housing development where school provision may lag behind house building. Such intensive use would be a temporary measure only, pending the extension of the school or the building of other new schools to serve the neighbourhood. The increased numbers would reduce, or eliminate entirely, the surplus workplaces which allow flexibility in use and choice of activity. This would tend to increase the amount of passive learning and to reduce the opportunities for informal practical work. Though designed for 240 pupils, this layout shows how the accommodation could be used intensively by eleven groups of 30 pupils making 330 in all. The organisation would need to be fairly formal, but the opportunity remains for five or even six of the groups to work quite informally. The work of four of the groups can spill over into the open shared areas where there is space and facilities for large-scale activities of a practical nature to develop. The mobility of the furniture also renders the science laboratory capable of considerable variation while the central drama/music space has great potential for imaginative use. Of the five closed spaces, one is technically equipped for language learning and another is tiered for discussion. In addition, there is a quiet book reference and study area available at all times. Although used intensively, it can still operate as a multi-activity unit with its own team of teachers formulating its own particular programme.

INTENSIVELY USED

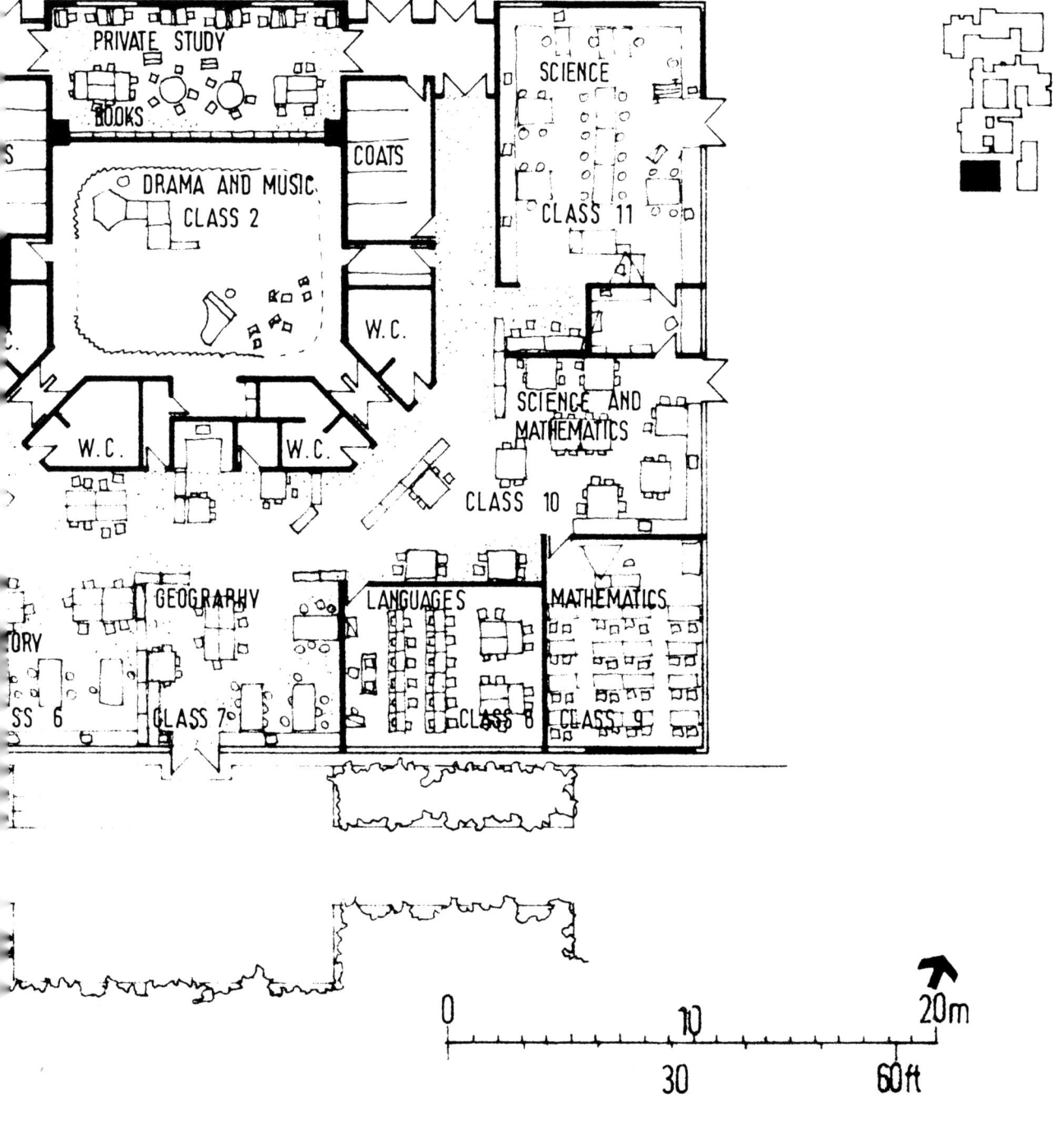

Plan 5 : AS A DEPARTMENT O

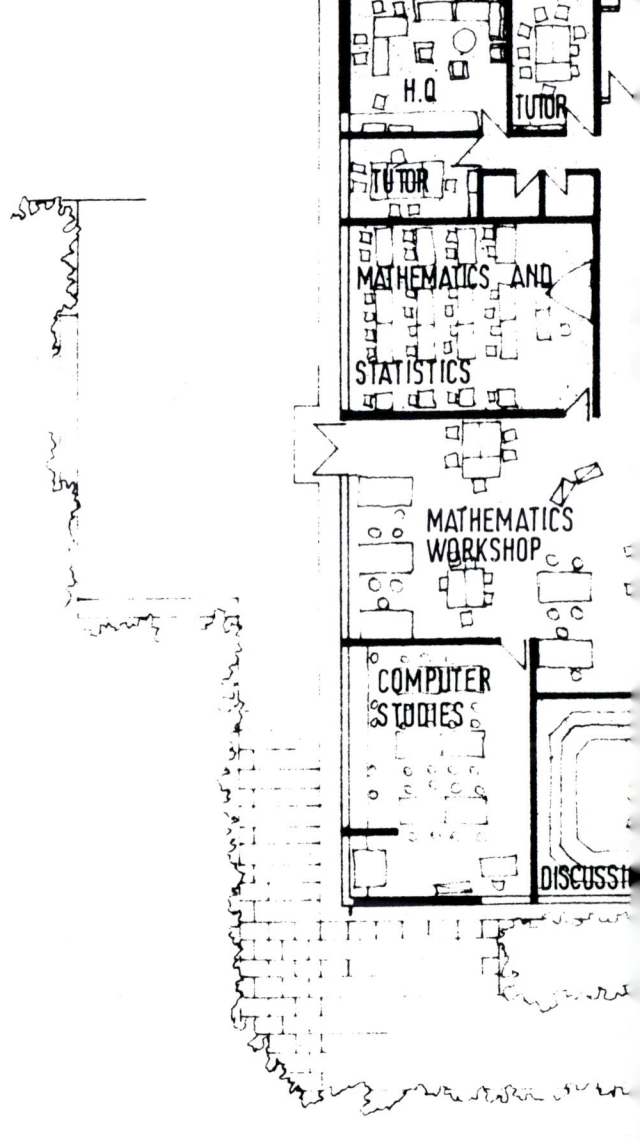

If on further re-organisation, the age range of the school became 13 to 18, instead of the present 11 to 18, and the lower school pupils were transferred elsewhere, then the unit would have to serve some other departmental function. One possibility is the creation of a department of modern studies. This is envisaged as an integrated course for senior students covering statistics and computer studies, economics, politics, ecology and biology (probably social biology). The plan involves very little physical change to the building. The central space is for lectures to large groups. There are five other closed spaces for various teaching and discussion groups which can be used either formally or informally. A central, open area provides book reference and ressources space with points at which tutors can be consulted or from which they can supervise particular surveys or projects. This is flanked by areas given over to mathematical studies and ecological investigations. There is access from the biology laboratory to animal houses, greenhouses, and gardens.

MODERN STUDIES (Upper School)

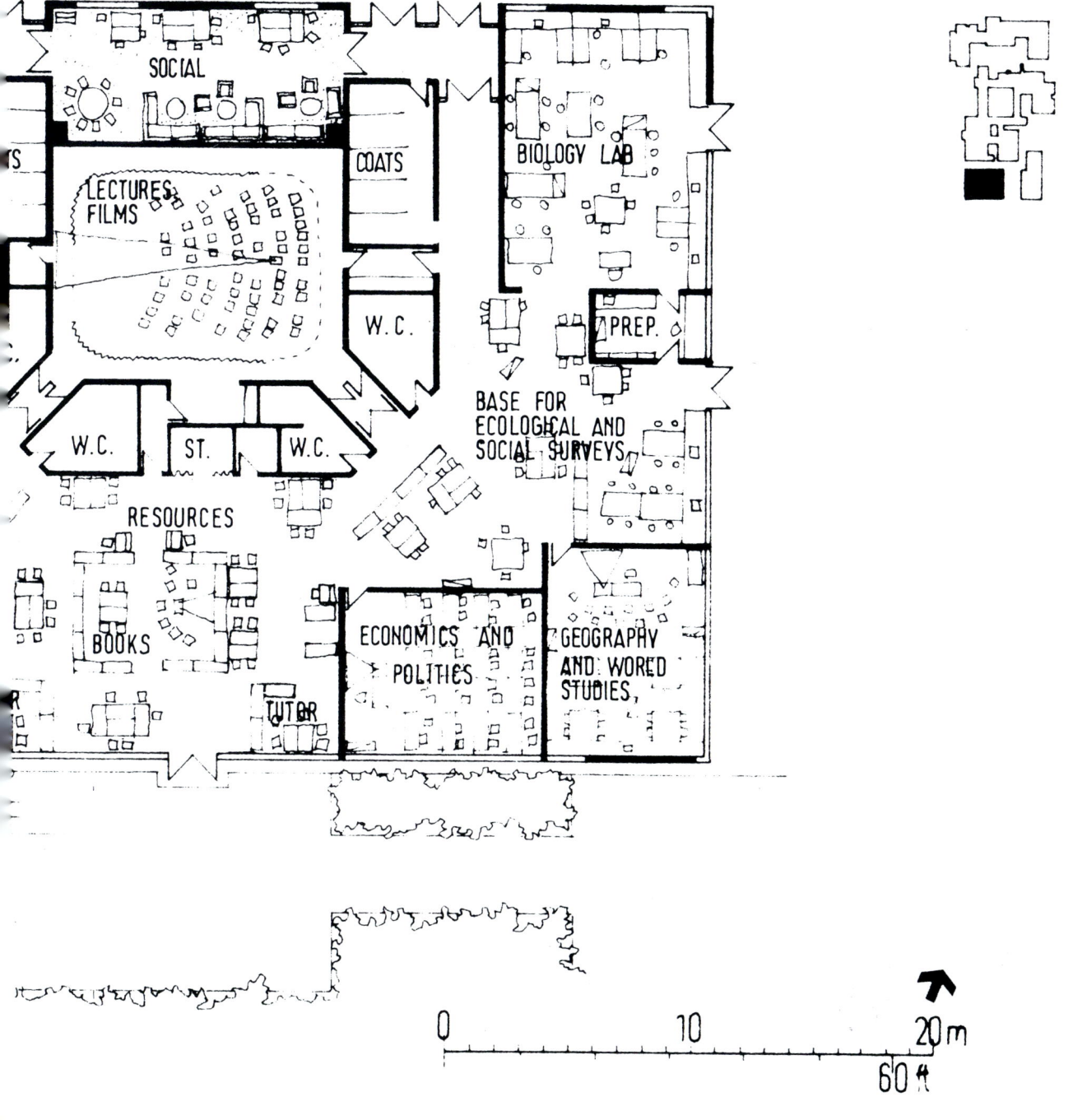

Plan 6 : AS A SCIENCE AN

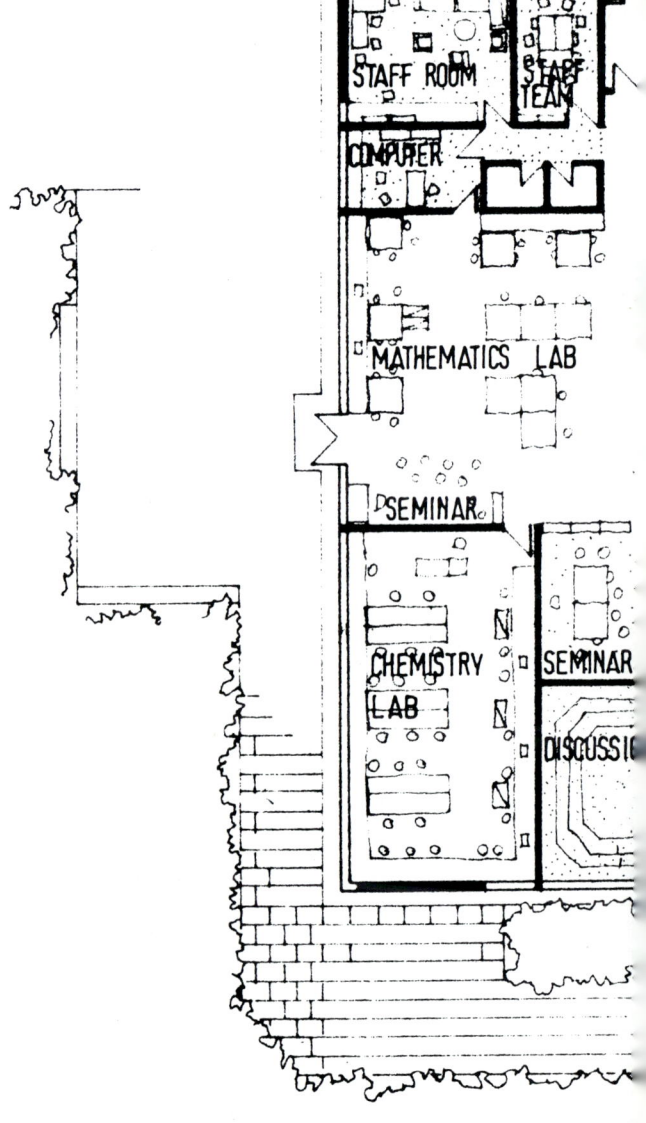

Here is another example of change of function due to re-organisation in which the unit becomes a science and mathematics department for older students. (An assumption is made that the existing science accommodation in the main science/home economics/craft department at the Maiden Erlegh School is needed to extend the craft facilities.) Adaptation of the unit for science purposes involves extensions to the existing services and some relocation of internal walls. The department includes all three main branches of science, the physical sciences and chemistry being accommodated in closed spaces. The general science and biology is planned more openly and has access to outside facilities used for rural science and horticultural courses. The main preparation and servicing room is centrally situated, convenient to all laboratories, and the main lecture room. The large central carpeted area includes information, resources and library facilities and a number of seminar or discussion spaces where tutors can meet small groups of students. A mathematics laboratory is developed in an extension to this area with a small computer room adjoining. A quiet space beyond the main lecture room is designed for mathematical group studies.

MATHEMATICS CENTRE (Upper School)

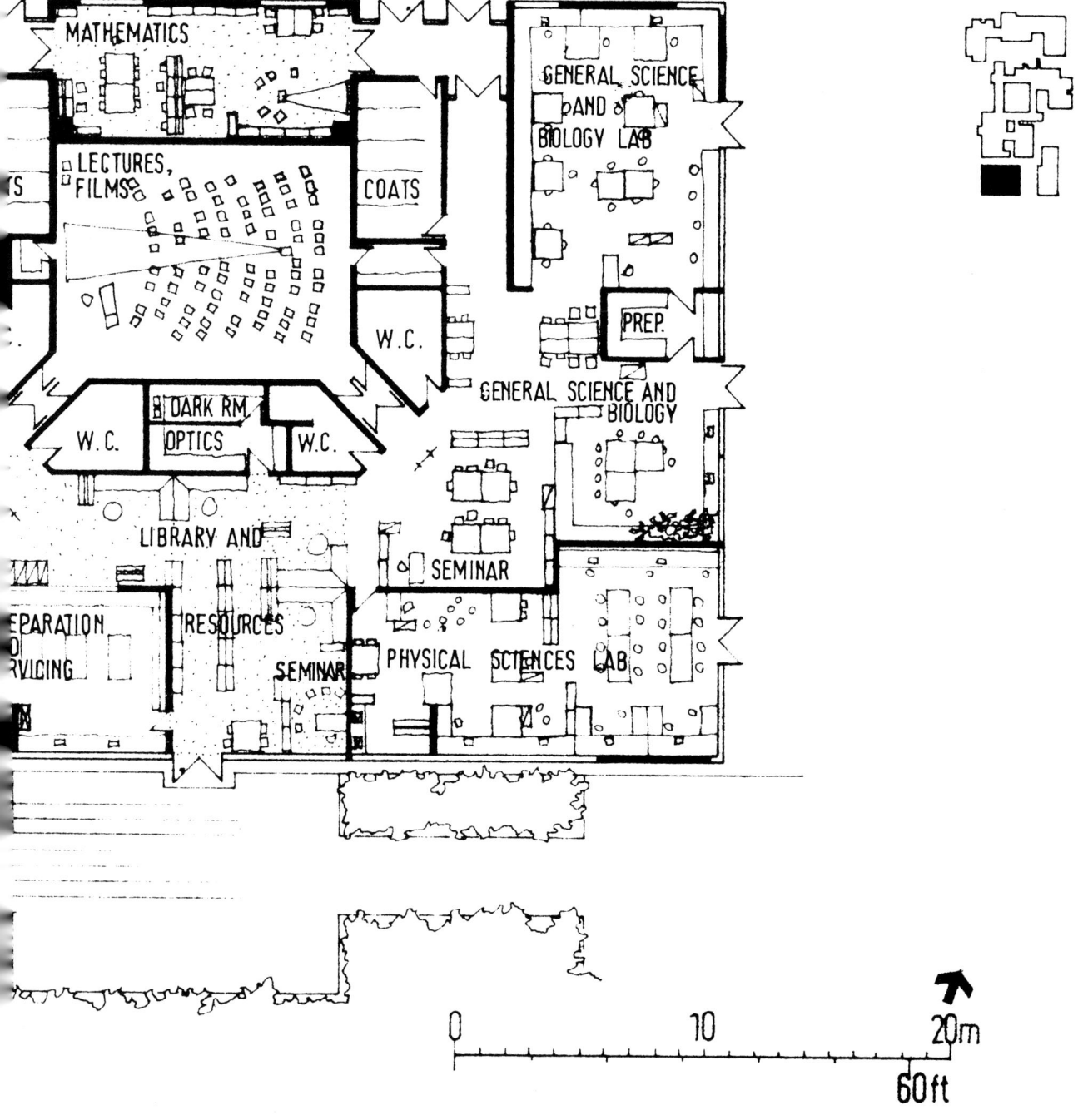

CASE STUDIES IN ADAPTABILITY

Bases for the Sucy-en-Brie and Arlington Exercises

17. These are theoretical exercises to test the adaptability to changed educational demands of two quite different school buildings in France and Canada respectively. In order to determine the limits of adaptability of these buildings, it was necessary to impose upon them educational requirements of an extreme, yet realistic, nature, demanding much more than the simple modifications to a building carried out to meet evolutionary changes. For this purpose it was decided to test the buildings against the educational and social demands of an English comprehensive school for 1,350 pupils aged 11 to 16 years. The French school was designed for 1,290 pupils of 11 to 15 years, a roughly comparable size. The Canadian school however was designed for 700 pupils aged 12 to 14 years but its floor area per pupil was greatly in excess of English and French standards, so that it offered substantial space for adaptation.

18. Such studies as these are not merely exercises in matching the teaching space requirements for an English comprehensive school with that provided in the French and Canadian schools respectively. They go deeper, for they are also concerned with fundamental differences in the role of school in society in these countries. In England, a school is regarded first of all as a living community of young people, and the teachers are as much concerned with their health, attitudes and social well-being as they are with progress in their curriculum studies. A comprehensive school is composed of many different types of people with differing aspirations, and drawn from different social backgrounds, and in school life they must learn to live together in unity and find common ground in the give and take of everyday affairs. The environment and facilities of the schools created by adaptation of the French and Canadian buildings should therefore actively promote community consciousness in the boys and girls through association and through the sharing of common interests and enterprises, and develop in them a capacity to meet change.

19. It should be emphasised at this point that no statutory curriculum requirements are imposed in England so that there are no fixed parameters round which the model may be structured, as there would be in many countries. Among educationists, however, there is a commonly accepted curriculum content and a degree of consensus as to the proportion of time given to particular areas of activity. However, much subjective judgement operates to produce variations in the balance of the curriculum. Subjects can be slanted in new directions to embrace new activities or integrated with other subjects to produce new curriculum areas. The English model, set out in the paragraphs and tables which follow, is only one of a number of possible variations of social and teaching organisation, all of which would have been acceptable at the present time. It is elaborated under the following five headings:

 i) Broad objectives. Social and curriculum organisation (based on Figure 1).
 ii) Table 1. Departmental arrangements.
 iii) Table 2. Estimate of number of workplaces required and average number of teachers engaged in each subject.
 iii) Table 3. Distribution of workplaces and social places.
 v) Table 4. Learning activities and groupings to be considered by the designers.

The model does not include a schedule of accommodation. Within the suggested distribution of workplaces and the table of learning activities and groupings, the design team has been free to work out its own space distribution, having regard to the broad objectives [i) above] outlined in paragraphs 20 to 23.

THE ENGLISH MODEL

Broad Objectives. Social and Curriculum Organisation (see Figure 1)

20. For social and pastoral purposes, the 1,350 pupils in the school community are sub-divided into a number of small communities with which individuals may more easily identify themselves and in the life of which each can make a significant contribution. The main divisions are as follows:

Lower School. Pupils of 11 and 12 years of age become members of the Lower School though they will share in the use of facilities outside their own territory. For pastoral purposes, design should permit the breaking down of the 540 pupils into still smaller groups. Shared general work areas, resource and study space should all be used in the social life of the department.

Upper School. This is for pupils of 13 years of age and onwards and is broken down into five communities of different sizes each based on a teaching centre. Each centre should have a core of social, study, resource and shared work areas on which the activities of the community will be based. It will be left for the headmaster and staff to determine the constitution of these communities e.g. whether by age, interests or other special objectives. They may, in fact, change from time to time.

Design should take into consideration the pastoral duties of some members of the staff by providing points or spaces from which they can function. The personal care and guidance of boys and girls is often a private matter for which a closed room is essential.

21. For learning purposes, the school is divided into a number of major teaching departments each of which will provide a base for a substantial community of the school. Designers should bear the following points in mind.

i) They are not to be thought of as narrow subject departments; each covers a broad spectrum of related studies and may include several conventional school subjects. Each will include a variety of learning activities and will have a core of space shared by all subjects.

ii) Nevertheless, these departments will provide for specialists to work in pursuit of their own subjects when this is required by the pupils—for example, to cope with special examination or vocational courses in physics, mathematics, history or technical subjects.

iii) The creation of very large departmental empires should be avoided as they tend to be sub-divided and then function as special subject departments.

iv) A department comprises spaces with special services, furniture and equipment designed for special teaching as well as shared space for general work. This latter space should be equipped with movable furniture to permit physical re-arrangement of the space to meet new educational needs.

v) The technical and physical education departments do not accommodate communities of the school. They need not be physically separated from other departments except insofar as their physical characteristics e.g. dust, fumes, impact noises, demand it.

vi) It can be assumed that the Upper School timetable is arranged in blocks of up to three periods (based on a 40-period week) permitting substantial groups to spend long periods of time within a department following a varied, individual or group programme.

22. Regarding staff accommodation, the following teaching posts can be considered to carry special responsibilities and require an office for each holder: Headmaster or Headmistress, Deputy Head, Head of Lower School, Director of Studies, four Heads of Upper School Departments and the Chief Librarian. A work space for departmental staff, linked with books and resources, is essential to the working of a department. This might incorporate the office of the Head of Department. Offices provided for pastoral purposes within the social areas would also serve as tutor rooms for general use by departments.

23. Dining facilities should be provided for at least 80 per cent of the pupils. If good social areas are provided then intensively used cafeteria dining arrangements are acceptable. If the dispersal of dining inhibits other social arrangements, then it is not to be preferred; for example, were dining in the Lower School to freeze a substantial section of its social space during the mid-day break, then it would tend to create more disciplinary problems than dispersal was trying to solve. Disciplinary problems are most acute at this period of the day when supervision is only thinly spread. Nevertheless, a large centralised dining area can be civilised by sub-division, thus creating a number of smaller dining groups. The staggering of the school day, particularly in the timetables of Lower and Upper Schools, enables dining space to be used over a longer period than would otherwise be the case.

30

Figure 1

Proposed Organisation of English Model School

School for 1,350 boys and girls. 11 to 16 years of age.
Annual entry 270 pupils. 5-year course.
Minimum teaching area[1] required : 5,171 m2.

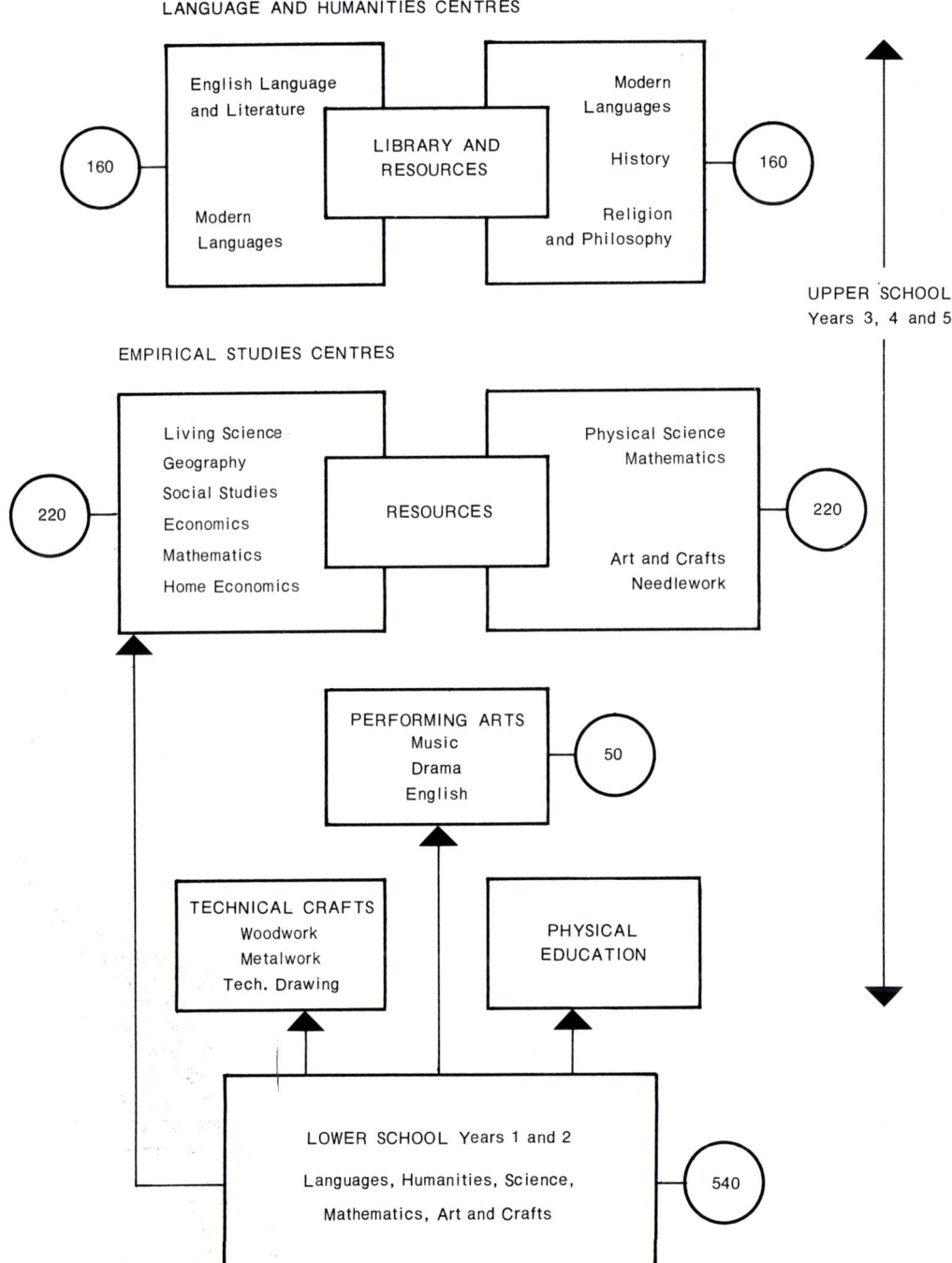

1. See paragraph 24(i).

Table 1

Departmental Arrangements.

---

1. TEACHING STAFF

Head	1
Deputy Head	1
Director of Studies	1
Head of Lower School	1
Upper School - Departmental Heads	4
Chief Librarian	1
Assistant Teachers	60

Six assistant teachers have special pastoral responsibilities within the social areas.

---

2. DEPARTMENTS

Lower School (540 pupils)

70 per cent of the curriculum will be followed within the Lower School area. Lower School shares in the use of the physical education, performing arts and technical accommodation.

Upper School (810 pupils)

Curriculum studies are grouped into four broad categories each forming a major department of the Upper School. These are:

Humanities

English
French
German or Russian
History—including Archeology
Religion and Philosophy
Human Affairs

Empirical Studies

Geography with Geology
Social Science and Economics
Mathematics
Science: i) Living Science
ii) Physical Science

The Arts

Music
Drama (theatre)
Arts (drawing, painting and design)
Crafts (pottery, modelling and other three-dimensional work, printing and needlework)
Physical Education
Indoor: Gymnastics
Dancing
Combat sports
Outdoor: Team games and athletics
Basket ball and tennis

Technology

Metalwork and Engineering (to include car maintenance)
Woodwork
Technical Drawing
Home Economics
Simple Building Processes (brick laying, tiling, concreting, etc.)

Table 2
Estimate of Number of Workplaces Required and Average Number of Teachers Engaged in Each Subject.

	Periods (out of 40)		Workplaces (out of 1,350)	Plus Margin for Flexibility in Organisation		Teachers
	1		2	3		4
				%		
English	5		168	10	185	8
Modern Languages	3		101	10	111	5
History	2		68	10	75	3
Religion and Philosophy	2		68	10	75	3
Geography, Social Science or Economics	3		101	10	111	4
Mathematics	5		168	10	185	8
Science	5		168	10	185	9
Music	2		68	10	75	3
Drama	1		34	25	42	1.5
Physical Education	2 indoor 2 outdoor		68 —	10 —	75 —	5
	Boys	Girls				
Art and Crafts	3	3	101	25	126	6
Needlework	—	2	34	30	44	1.5
Home Economics	—	3	51	30	66	4
Wood and Metalwork	4	—	68	30	88	5
Technical Drawing	1	—	17	30	22	1

Notes
i) In addition to the above there should be at least 135 workplaces in Library/Study/Resources areas (10 per cent of pupils).
ii) Subjects in which a variety of specially equipped workplaces are required (e.g. metalwork) need a more generous margin for flexibility than do general subjects. Hence the differences in column 3.
iii) Column 4 should be loosely interpreted. Some teachers will engage in two or more subjects and may even divide their time between departments. Of the 67 teachers, 8 to 10 will be free during any period.
iv) The separation of boys and girls practical activities is merely to reach a statistical answer. Some boys may take cookery and some girls woodwork, but for average purposes, the periods as shown, plus a generous margin of places for flexibility in organisation, should cover all eventualities.

In the following table, the workplaces estimated in Table 2 are distributed among the various departments. In the past, secondary school departments have been small, tight, subject-centred enclaves e.g. English, Modern Languages, History, Geography, Mathematics, Science, Home Economics, Workshop Crafts, Art, Music and so on. They have varied considerably in their demands for floor area e.g. in the same school a History Department with an area of 150 square metres (three teachers) and a Science Department with 600 square metres (nine teachers). It is now becoming more usual to sub-divide a school into fewer departments each having considerable autonomy and developing combined courses in a number of related subjects. This results in a spread of special facilities rather than concentrations of them, and departments with a variety of learning modes and of environmental conditions. Such departments cover substantial territories and involve the juxtaposition of a variety of learning and living activities. They are flexible in use, adaptable within themselves and often completely interchangeable (as at Maiden Erlegh).

Table 3
The English Model. Distribution of Workplaces and Social Places.

	Humanities I	Humanities II	Empirical Studies I	Empirical Studies II	Performing Arts	Physical Education Centre	Technical Centre	Lower School
English	90				25			70
Modern Languages	36	35						40
History		45						30
Religion and Philosophy		45						30
Geography, etc.			67					44
Mathematics			35	80				70
Science			54	79				60
Art and Crafts				90				36
Needlework				44				
Home Economics			66					
Music					75			
Drama					42			
Wood and Metalwork							88	
Technical Drawing							22	
Physical Education						68 indoor 68 outdoor		
Library, Resources and Study	30	30	10	10				30
Social Places	160	160	220	220	50			540

Notes
i) The social communities in Empirical Studies centres I and II appear large but the centres themselves cover generous floor areas and such numbers of pupils should be easily absorbed. It is most desirable that each community of 220 should be broken down within its own centre so as to avoid undue concentrations of people.

ii) The Lower School copes with 70 per cent of its own curriculum which means that 360 to 400 pupils are being taught there at any one time. But 540 pupils are to be based in the department so that it is important to spread them in social and general work areas.

Table 4
Learning Activities and Groupings to be Considered.

ACTIVITIES	GROUPINGS
Listening and looking.	In groups of 30 in 1st, 2nd and 3rd years and about 20 in 4th and 5th years. This might be normal teaching or television viewing.
Reading.	Individual and informal as well as in small teacher-directed groups.
Discussion.	Groups of 20-30 are common but more facility needed for small discussion groups e.g. up to 10 pupils.
Writing and studying at a table.	In groups of 30 or about 20 with a teacher.
Calculation and theoretical problem solving.	Considerable individual study as well as group work.
Investigating—collecting, arranging, systematising, classifying, taking to pieces, etc., e.g. in Geography, Geology, Natural History, Archeology and Social Science (compiling charts, distribution maps, etc.).	In groups of 30 or about 20. These are often sub-divided into small groups of 3 to 5 pupils each engaged in a particular aspect of a study. Such work can be entirely individual.
Experimenting with services and apparatus — in all branches of science	Generally in groups of 25 to 30. Pupils often experiment in pairs or break up into groups of 5 or 6 depending on the scale and complexity of the experiment.
— in Mathematics (lectures and demonstrations by teachers are an integral part of this work).	Often by a whole group of 25 to 30 working at grouped experiments (e.g. in mechanics, dynamics or setting up models) or by individuals withdrawing from theoretical groups (e.g. using devices for measuring, estimating quantities, navigation, etc.).

ACTIVITIES	GROUPINGS
Practice in the Arts Drawing, painting and design (lectures in the fine arts, discussions, incidental use of slides and films are all an essential part of this work).	Work generally organised in groups of 20 to 30 but the activities themselves are largely individual.
Pottery, modelling, three-dimensional constructions, printing, textiles, etc. (The skills and interests of the teachers themselves often determine the crafts to be pursued.)	Organised in groups of 20 to 30. Sometimes it is possible to engage a whole group in a single craft but more often it is sub-divided into a number of groups engaged in different crafts.
Needlework—this now goes beyond the acquisition of skills necessary to a needle-woman and is moving into the realms of fashion. Activities cover designing, drafting, cutting out, sewing, creative work with fabrics, displaying and modelling, buying accessories, etc.	In groups or 30 in lower classes, often reduced to 15 or 20 in upper classes.
Choral singing.	Generally in groups of 30.
Playing musical instruments.	Individual practice. Group learning and group practice e.g. six or seven violonists working together. Orchestral practice with 40-50 instrumentalists.
Listening to music.	Group listening through tape deck, etc.; individual listening.
Theoretical studies in music.	In groups of 20 to 30.
Spontaneous drama and play reading.	Groups of 20 to 30. This activity may also emerge in language teaching.
Creating the illusions of theatre play production.	In groups of 30 in the Lower School probably in small groups of up to 15 in the Upper School.
Dancing and dramatic movement.	In groups of 20 to 30.
Using Physical Skills Agility and strength training. Practice in games skills, combat sports, athletics and team games.	Generally in groups of 30, sub-divided into activity groups.
Technical Skills Cooking and cleaning.	Basic groups of 16 pupils. The number may rise to 20 occasionally. Pupils often work in pairs or in groups of 3 or 4.
Maintaining the services of a home. Retail shopping and consumer studies.	Facilities for demonstration to groups of up to 20 are needed.
Normal metalwork processes (shaping/beating, brazing, welding, forging).	In groups of 15 to 20 pupils, often sub-divided into craft groups.
Simple engineering and car maintenance. Work with plastics.	Groups of 5 or 6 pupils.
Working in wood. Simple building processes of concreting, brick laying, tiling, etc. (facilities outside).	In groups of 15 to 20 pupils. Small groups of 5 or 6 pupils.
Technical drawing.	Generally taken in groups of about 20. Smaller special groups may emerge in the Upper School.

Design Decisions or Assumptions

24. The following constraints were accepted at the outset of the design work and applied to both the Sucy-en-Brie and Arlington exercises.

i) The norms applicable to school building in England were observed. These governed:

— physical standards, based on English Building Regulations, School Premises Regulations and Department of Education and Science (DES) Regulations and Guidelines (among these standards is the "minimum teaching area", an important concept in English school design and one which does not prescribe detailed floor area requirements but demands a minimum total teaching area depending on numbers and ages of pupils; teaching area does not include area devoted to circulation, administration, dining, kitchens and plant);

— environmental standards likewise based —but not unrealistically i.e. where achievement of 90 per cent of any required standard costs half of that to reach 100 per cent, then 90 per cent is considered acceptable;

— educational standards and requirements generally, including normal community and pastoral facilities. (Of special significance in the observation of these norms and guidelines is the expressed desirability of natural daylighting in every space or at least a "view out" to the exterior surroundings of the building. Where, however, areas are inevitably either totally internal or the view out absent or very indirect then the standard of internal finishes should be increased, the lighting boosted by, for example, the use of spotlights and/or extra pendant fittings, and the area generally treated as "special" to compensate.)

ii) Existing walls and services were to be used as far as possible, provided they did not unduly inhibit the English model. No major structural alterations were to be considered.

iii) Alterations to plumbing and drainage were to be kept to a minimum. This included the sanitary fittings provision (so that W.C.'s, etc., would generally be retained where they were even though ideally they might be, say, more dispersed throughout the building). Further assumptions were made which were particular to each design

exercise. These are detailed below in the relevant commentaries on the work undertaken.

SUCY-EN-BRIE

The School as Existing
(Plans 7 to 10 inclusive)

25. The Collège d'enseignement secondaire (C.E.S.) at Sucy-en-Brie, France, is for 1,200 pupils aged 11 to 15 years. It also includes accommodation for 90 pupils of the same age range who require special educational treatment. Sucy is a small township some 20 kilometers south east of Paris and the school serves a new residential area. It is built on a pleasant, open site which includes amenity areas as well as residential accommodation for some members of the staff. The main building is on three storeys and in addition there is a basement area which accommodates separately the unit for special educational treatment. The workshop serving this unit is also at the basement level. Each floor of the main building comprises four platforms, linked by staircases and lavatory blocks as shown in Figure 2. These platforms offered interesting possibilities for adaptation within themselves, while combinations of them presented possibilities for creating the several departments required by the English model. The uniformity of design, the limited distribution of services and the unsuitability of the acoustic conditions for the more fluid arrangements of space required by the model, all presented the designers with special adaptation problems. The variety and proportion of practical facilities in the school also fell short of the requirements of the English model.

26. The school was built in 1971-72 and reflects the concern of the French Ministry of Education to ensure that school buildings are so planned and constructed as to be in some measure adaptable to new educational demands, whatever form they might take. The constructional answer to the problems set by this pre-occupation was seen to lie in the adoption of a structural frame with spans of the order of 7 to 9 metres, and non-load-bearing internal partitions which offer the possibility of future repositioning. The identification and isolation of certain "fixed" elements which are unlikely to change e.g. staircases, lavatories and certain types of specialist accommodation, would also assist these adaptations.

Plan 7 : SUCY-EN-BRIE AS EXISTING BASEMENT LEVEL

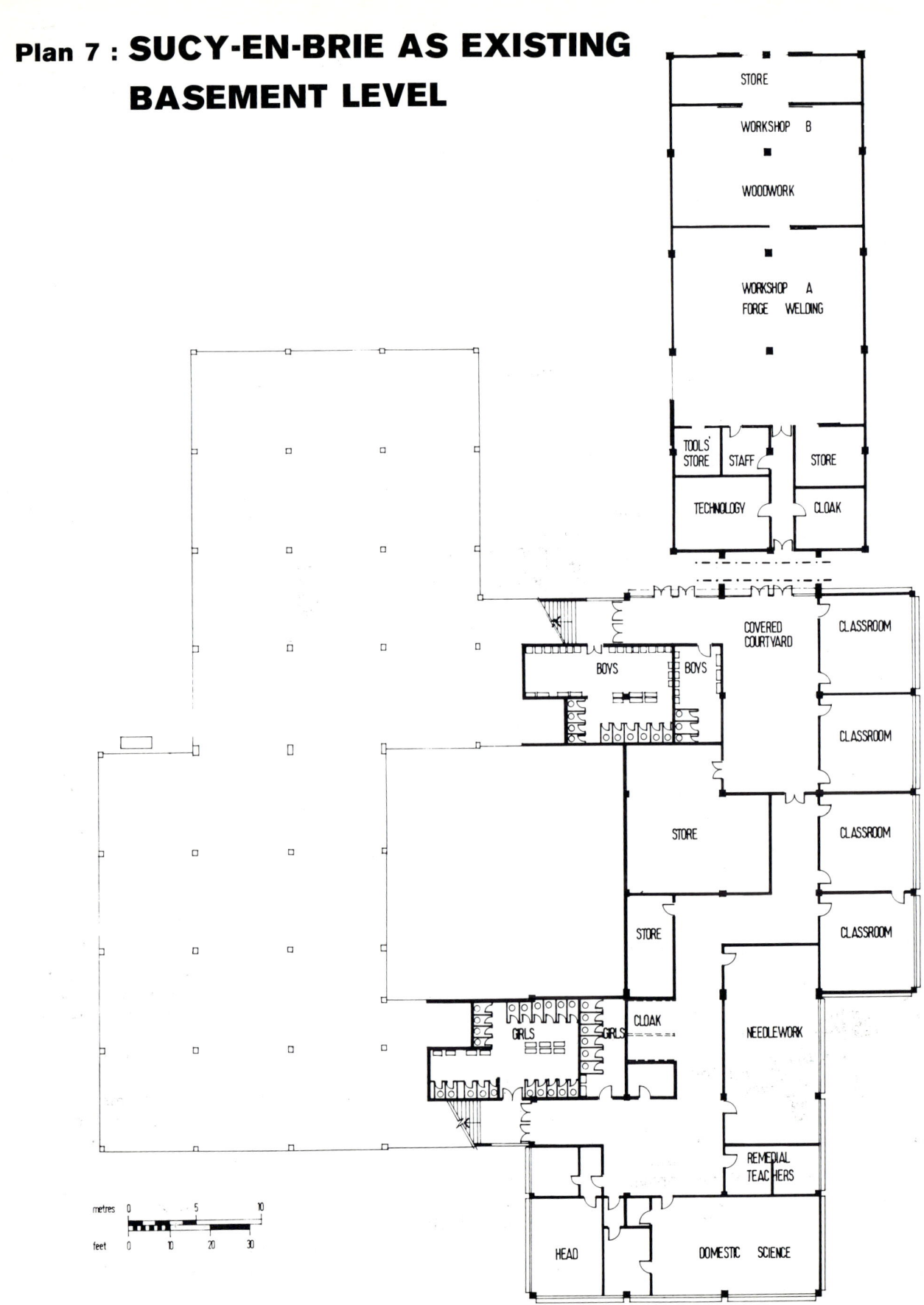

Plan 8 : SUCY-EN-BRIE AS EXISTING ENTRANCE LEVEL

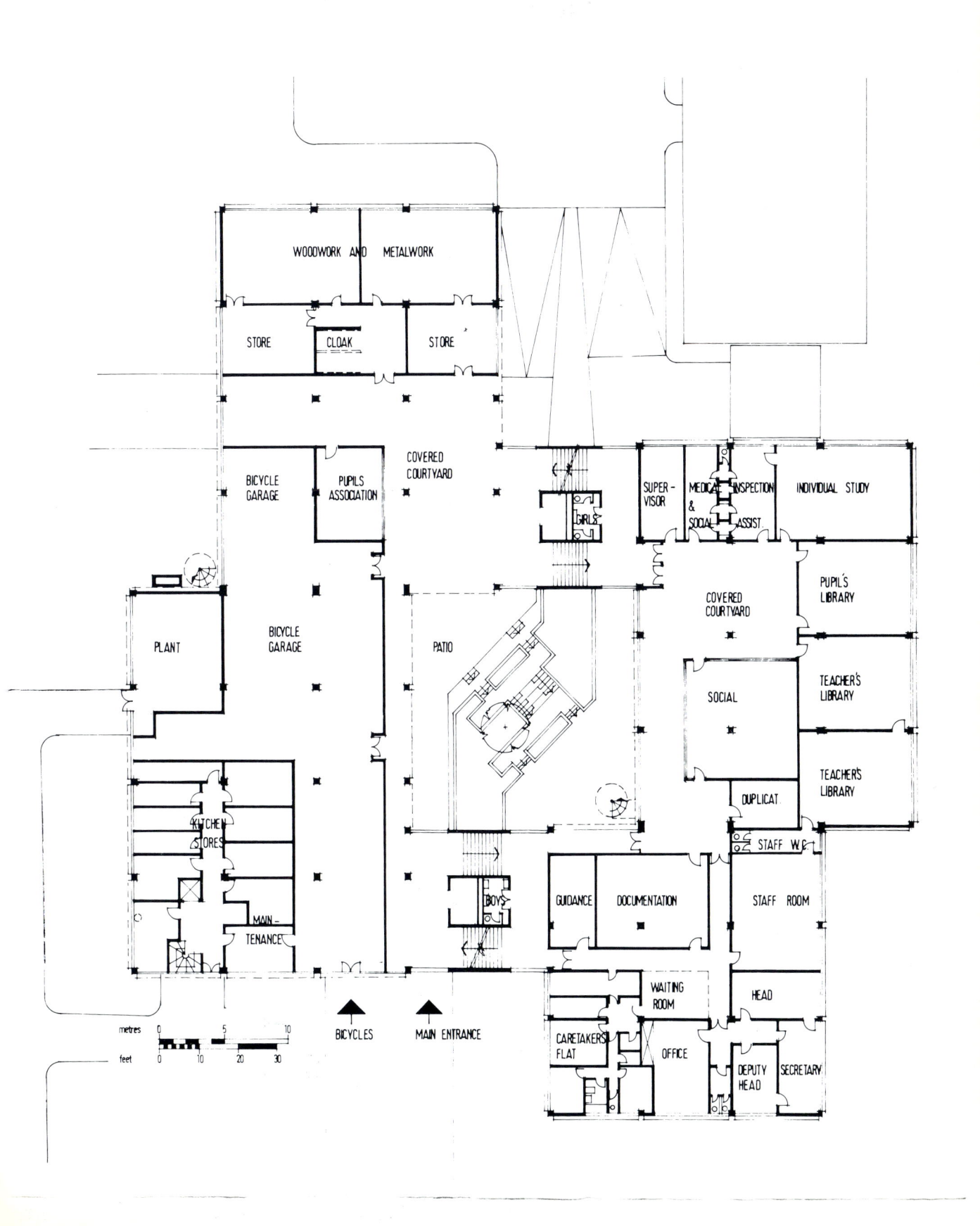

Plan 9 : SUCY-EN-BRIE AS EXISTING FIRST FLOOR LEVEL

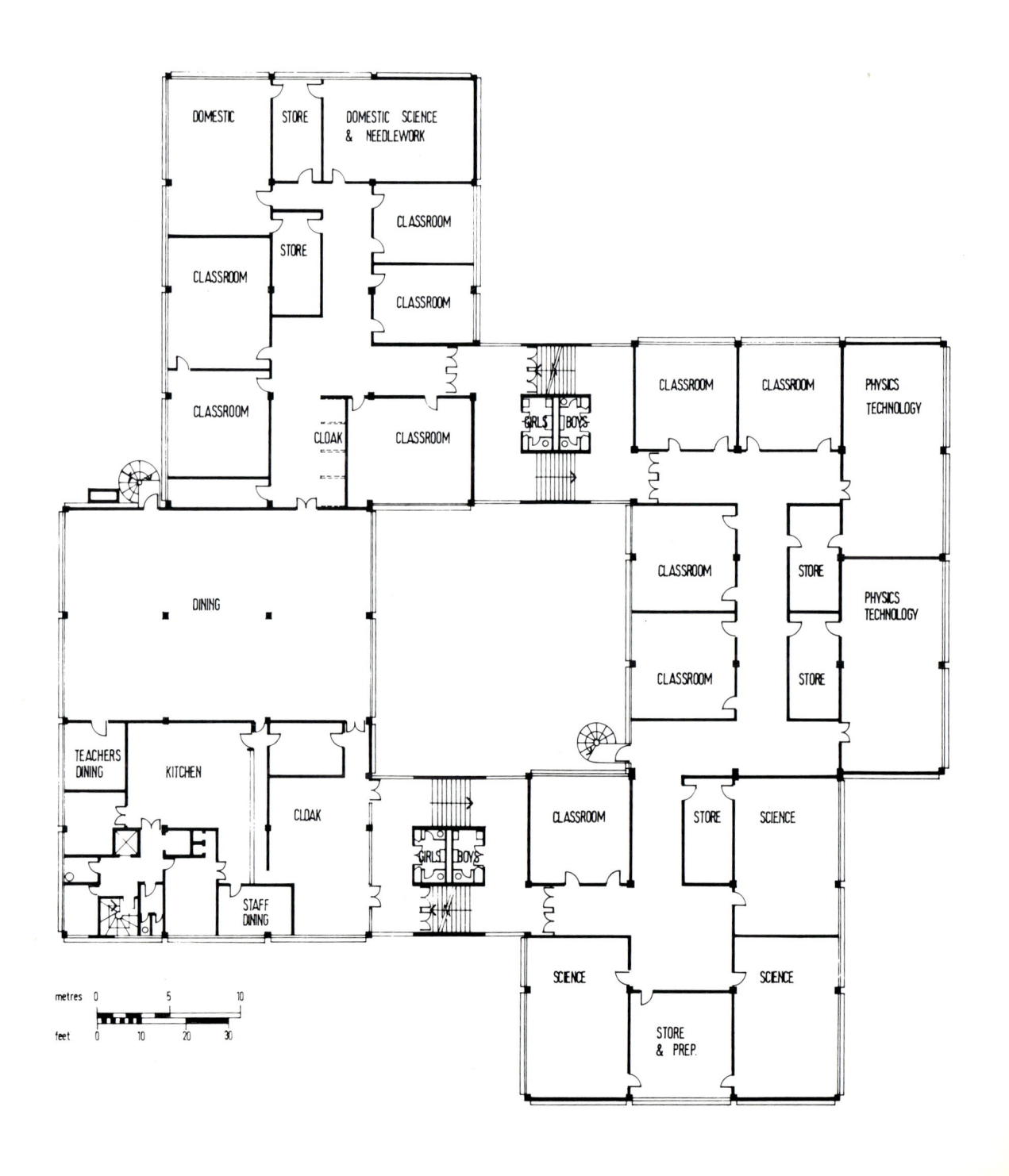

Plan 10 : **SUCY-EN-BRIE AS EXISTING SECOND FLOOR LEVEL**

27. In the case of Sucy-en-Brie, which is one of a number of schools designed and built by a joint architect/contractor team in response to these Ministry requirements, a 1.80 metre planning module is adopted with a square structural bay size of 7.20 metres. Columns are concrete and the floors two-way concrete slabs in the form of 0.90 metre square grid egg-crate construction. There is a clear distinction between the accommodation considered adaptable to future change i.e. that provided by a series of platforms sized 3×3 or 3×4 structural bays (21.60 metres square or 21.60 metres×28.80 metres) and the accommodation containing the fixed elements i.e. staircases, lavatories and vertical service runs, grouped in blocks and positioned to serve and link the platforms. Internal partitioning is in lightweight reconstituted timber panels and can be positioned and repositioned anywhere on the 0.90 metre ceiling grid to give any required configuration of spaces.

Fitting the Model into the Building

28. A school concept cannot be entirely fluid and is therefore not something which can be just poured into a rigid container. It has already been made clear in paragraph 19 that the comprehensive school model represents but one of a number of possibilities, all of which would be acceptable in England at the present time. Some modification of its requirements is to be expected in attempting to fit it into an existing building. These modifications to the brief are not to be regarded as a measure of "inadaptability" on the part of the building. The fact that the English model has been loosely and comfortably fitted into the physical envelope provided by the Sucy-en-Brie building, with only minor modification, is due partly to the flexibility of interpretation inherent in the brief itself. Undue precision in the demands of a brief increase the problems of adaptation and may finally render a solution impossible.

29. The first step was to examine the units of floor area available for adaptation as teaching accommodation. The building offers two sizes of platform as follows:

    a)   28.80m × 21.60m = 622m^2
    b)   21.60m × 21.60m = 466m^2

and the typical distribution of platforms on each floor is as shown in Figure 2 below. School departments are most conveniently created from single platforms or from two adjoining platforms. While three adjoining platforms on the same floor might be re-designed to provide a large department, the separation of two of them by the fixed staircase elements imposes some inconvenience upon their day-to-day running. In some circumstances, this arrangement might have to be accepted. Floor areas available for the most convenient departmental arrangements are therefore:

    (a)+(a)   1,244m^2
    (a)+(b)   1,088m^2
    (a)   622m^2
    (b)   466m^2

Figure 2

Typical Distribution of Platforms on Each Floor at Sucy-en-Brie

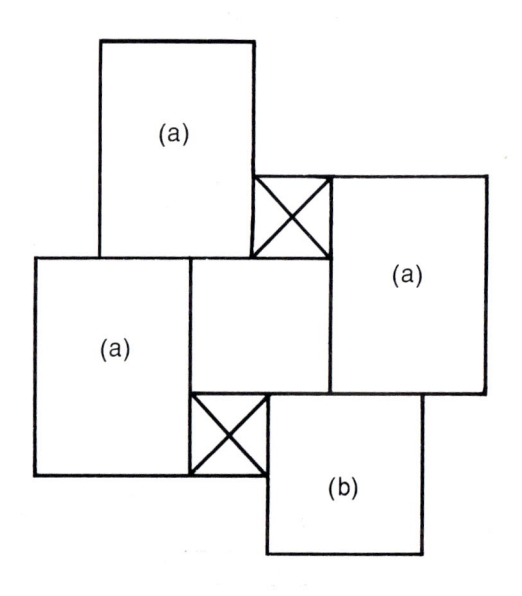

30. Exceptional to this is the basement at present used for the 90 children with special educational requirements and also the technical centre. Here, *(a)+(b)* becomes 1,988m^2 less the lavatory accommodation for the whole school. The technical centre provides 518m^2 (14.40m × 36.00m).

31. The second step was to calculate roughly the areas required by the various departments to test whether they could be accommodated within the platforms or in multiples of them as suggested in paragraph 29. Three examples of these are:

Humanities II

Number of Pupils per Subject	Breakdown by Area of Workplaces		Total Areas
	1.858m² per Pupil	2.787m² per Pupil	
35—Modern Languages	35	—	65.030
45—History	20	25	106.835
45—Religious Studies and Philosophy	30	15	97.545
30—Resources	30	—	55.740
160—Social Centre (at 0.929m² per pupil)			148.640
			473.790

This breakdown shows that it might be possible to design the Humanities II in a platform size *(a)*.

Empirical Studies I

Number of Pupils per Subject	Breakdown by Area of Workplaces			Total Areas
	1.858m² per Pupil	2.787m² per Pupil	4.645m² per Pupil	
67—Geography	30	37	—	158.859
45—Mathematics	25	20	—	102.190
54—Science	—	54	—	150.498
66—Home Economics	—	30	36	250.830
10—Private Study	10	—	—	18.580
220—Social Centre (at 0.929m² per pupil)				204.380
				885.337

This breakdown shows that *(a)+(b)* will scarcely be sufficient as some 371.60m² of circulation and storage space will be necessary for this amount of teaching space; hence *(a)+(a)* is the only possibility.

Lower School

Number of Pupils per Subject	Breakdown by Area of Workplaces		Total Areas
	1.858m² per Pupil	2.787m² per Pupil	
70—English	40	30	157.930
40—Modern Languages	40	—	74.320
30—History	30	—	55.740
30—Religion and Philosophy	30	—	55.740
44—Geography	20	24	104.048
70—Mathematics	40	30	157.930
60—Science	—	60	167.220
36—Art and Crafts	—	36	100.332
30—Resources and Study	30	—	55.740
540—Social Centre (at 0.465m² per pupil)			251.100
			1,180.100

Allowing for circulation and storage of 464.50m², a total 1,644.60m² is required for the Lower School. Making allowances for adapting an existing area (10 per cent) it required *(a)+(a)+(b)* — a fifth departmental arrangement.

32. The following conclusions can be drawn from the above:

i) The building offers five possible department sizes in terms of their floor areas, plus the technical department which presents some difficulty in its incorporation.

ii) Except for the two large Empirical Studies Departments, the English model can be contained within the platform arrangements.

iii) The total floor area required by these two departments is roughly *3(a) + 2(b)*. Hence some modification is called for while still maintaining their objectives and their multidisciplinary characteristics. What suggests itself is two main departments of *(a)+(b)* and an associated smaller department *(a)*.

Adjustment to the Model (see Figure 3)

33. During the architect/educationist dialogue which was maintained throughout the design exercise, the English model was inevitably adapted to the physical constraints of the Sucy-en-Brie building so that a second stage model evolved. This was no less valid as a school than the first but modified according to the particular circumstances. A continuous process of decision-making was necessary regarding the limitations and conditions within which the design team would operate. This is briefly recorded below and followed by a summary of the key decisions and modifications to the model that emerged.

34. The model divided the school into a Lower School for years 1 and 2 and an Upper School for years 3, 4 and 5. Whereas there tends to be considerable specialisation in the work of the latter requiring a departmental structure of organisation, the former finds greatest advantage in closely integrated facilities which allow courses and studies to cross the usual subject framework. Thus the Lower School accommodation is of a more general nature covering the whole of the curriculum except for work in physical education, music, drama and technical crafts. These latter facilities would become too fragmented and less effective were they to be sub-divided.

35. Both Lower and Upper Schools sub-divide further into a series of units within which the pastoral aspects of English educational practice can operate. Each unit becomes the home base for a community of teachers and pupils and the centre of their social life.

Lower School

36. Space distribution within Sucy-en-Brie presented difficulties in accommodating the pedagogical model for the Lower School. It was thought desirable to keep the Lower School at ground level as far as possible for two main reasons: first, to moderate the effects of transfer from a small primary school to a comparatively enormous secondary school and second, because the natural exuberance and energy of pupils of this age demands that they should be in close proximity to the outside play areas. If design compelled these young pupils to travel through the rest of the school to their own bases they could have felt intimidated by the sheer size of the establishment as a whole.

37. The Lower School is the largest unit of accommodation in the school and the platform sizes and their inter-relationship dictated its sub-division into three groups on three platforms. Around each social base it was necessary to arrange the facilities so that each base maintained its own identity yet operated as a part of a cohesive unit though on different levels. The basement level Blocks A and B and entrance level Block B appeared as the most suitable platforms and areas.

38. The existing services determined the positions of the science laboratories which were linked with the mathematics section around a social area in the basement Block A. The most desirable subject groupings were considered to be science and mathematics, languages and humanities, art and crafts. Languages and humanities fitted well into the basement Block B as did art and crafts into the entrance level Block B. One problem was with the social area in the science and mathematics group where the already tight areas were further diminished by the coat hanging space needed.

39. It was hoped that the full storey height distance between the languages and humanities section and the art and crafts section would not prevent the three platforms from being used as one complete lower school. It would certainly have been preferable if all three could have been on the same level but by spreading the practical areas over two floors it was hoped to minimise this disadvantage.

Upper School

40. It was found that the two humanities departments combined would fit into two large platforms but neither empirical studies department would fit into a combination of two platforms. Each would have too much space if it were spread over three platforms, and, in any case, there was an insufficient number of platforms available to do this. The pratical course of action was therefore to review the facilities and attempt to create a third empirical studies or some other department.

41. This was achieved by removing the home economics from one of the empirical studies departments and combining it with needlework taken from the other, thus creating a new department of home and fashion studies. Although this might be considered as an educationally retrogressive step in isolating these subjects it is nonetheless well established that they can operate well together as a grouping of "domestic science". By positioning this newly created empirical studies department in Block C (first floor) links can easily be established with the main school kitchen and dining room (Block D, first floor). Food can easily be trolleyed from one to the other and provision made in the base for alternative catering—for example, the easy incorporation of a snack-bar in the social area. It was important to link needlework with art and crafts and this has been done by positioning the art and craft facilities across the stair tower in neighbouring Block B.

42. The first empirical studies department is therefore revised to consist of the art and craft accommodation in Block B, a mathematics laboratory and computor studies space in the same block, and a suite of physical science accommodation in Block A, where science laboratories and services already exist. The demonstration room in the science area will be shared by all subjects taken in the department. The department includes two social areas, the smaller one of which is located in the science area.

43. Two humanities departments and the second empirical studies department remain to be housed. As the former need two larger platforms and the latter includes living science laboratories, the two units establish themselves on the second floor in Blocks C and D, and in Blocks A and B respectively.

44. By centralising the library and resources centre, the rest of Blocks C and D are available for the smaller group rooms to be placed around the perimeter, partially enclosing the social areas which double up as extra work

Figure 3

Accommodating the English Model

Basis of decisions within the platform structure of the French building

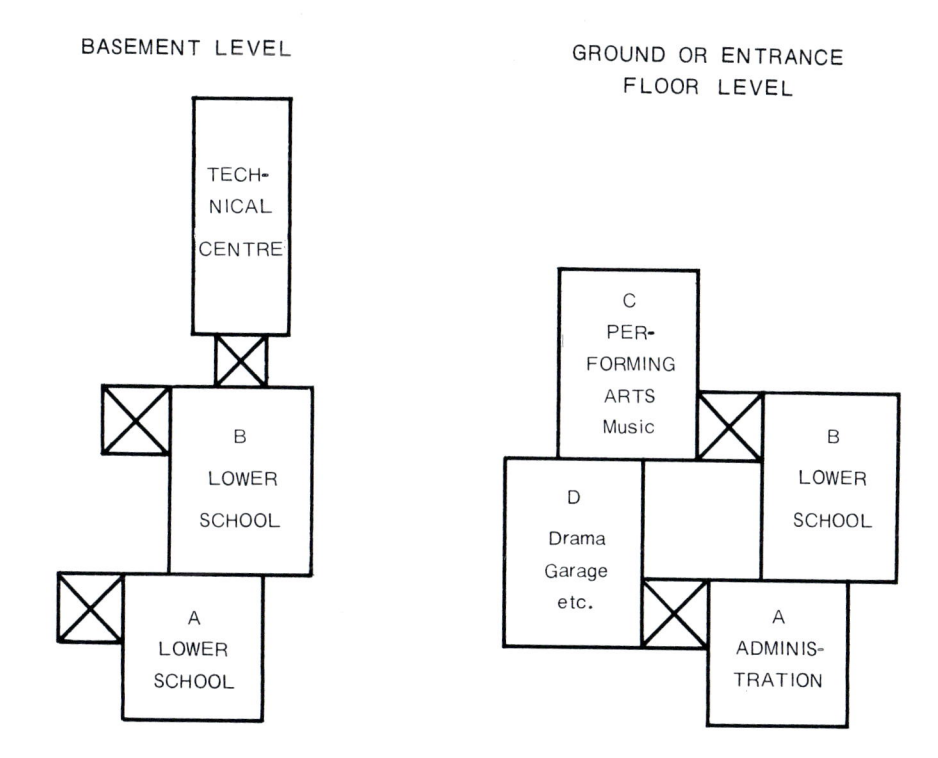

BASEMENT LEVEL

- TECHNICAL CENTRE
- B LOWER SCHOOL
- A LOWER SCHOOL

GROUND OR ENTRANCE FLOOR LEVEL

- C PERFORMING ARTS Music
- B LOWER SCHOOL
- D Drama Garage etc.
- A ADMINISTRATION

FIRST FLOOR LEVEL

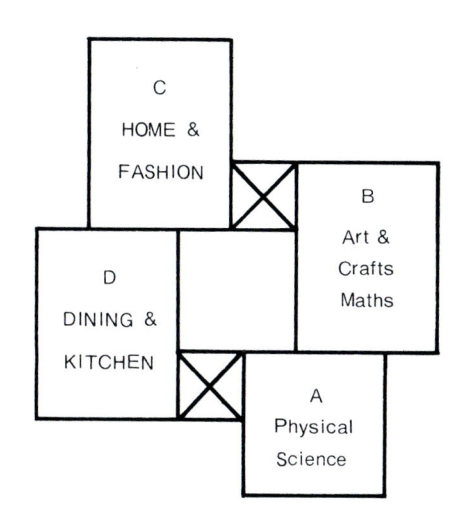

- C HOME & FASHION
- B Art & Crafts Maths
- D DINING & KITCHEN
- A Physical Science

A + B : EMPIRICAL STUDIES II

SECOND FLOOR LEVEL

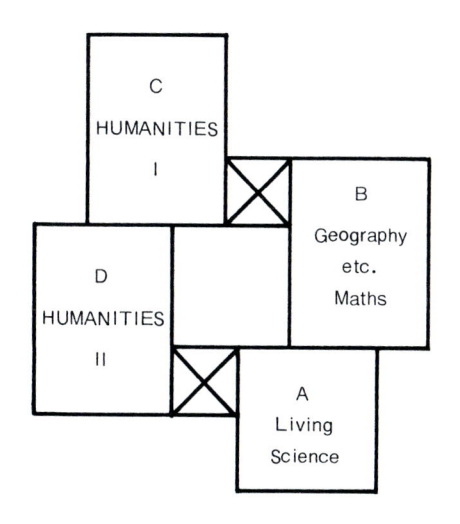

- C HUMANITIES I
- B Geography etc. Maths
- D HUMANITIES II
- A Living Science

A + B : EMPIRICAL STUDIES I

area in practice wherever necessary. A staff team room is included in this unit off the library and resources area for members of staff to discuss joint teaching projects.

45. The second empirical studies department fitted into Blocks A and B allowing the technical drawing room to be included. As in the other empirical studies department, an extra, small social resources base has been included among the living sciences laboratories to create a "humanised" area. As this is a totally internal space, it will need extra lighting and compensatory treatment, as defined in paragraph 24 i).

Shared Facilities

46. Facilities shared by the Lower School and the Upper School are the performing arts, technical crafts, some art and craft, dining and the main library and resources centre. It was thought desirable to position these between the two sections of the school. The existing "atelier" was used for technical crafts for four main reasons: first, its direct access to the outside covered paved areas would encourage projects on, for instance, vehicles or boats; second, the materials needed in this unit are bulkier than those used elsewhere and direct access to the service road allows the most convenient delivery; third, the expense of re-servicing any other area with phase electrical power supply would be avoided; and fourth, the strengthening of floors in any other area to take the load of the machinery involved would be unnecessary.

47. The floor area of the "atelier" and its position in relation to the service road, covered and uncovered paved areas determined the layout of the general, woodwork, metalwork and engineering workshops and their shared storage space. The covered link with the main school building was envisaged as an extension for general crafts. However, the area of the "atelier" and the limitations on its layout due to its plan form, existing masonry walls, columns and convector heaters did not allow room for the technical drawing office. It was therefore decided to incorporate this in the upper school mathematics accommodation as a shared-use facility.

48. Both the large drama studio and the large music studio needed to be positioned where they least disturb the rest of the school. In addition, they are both larger than any existing space in the school. It was decided to put them, and the rest of the performing arts facilities, on the entrance level in Blocks C and D using some of the cycle garage area.

The drama studio was located beneath the dining room where it would not upset any teaching. This gave easy access from the outside, particularly useful in the event of public performances.

49. It was decided to maintain a covered link through the entrance level Block C to the east stair tower. This divided the performing arts centre into two areas, one for music and one for drama. The area cut off to the east of Block C suited the music department's requirements and includes a study/reference space. The drama section provides the main social base for the 50 pupils in the performing arts centre. The large drama studio was then determined but, unavoidably, with a column intruding into the centre of the space. This was envisaged as having a perimeter lighting gallery and the facility to draw curtains around the whole room, if and when required. The storage also had to be split owing to the position of the boiler house. A group room was also provided and a green room for changing and making-up.

50. Dining was retained in its existing position as were the kitchen and kitchen stores. This left the shared facility of some art and crafts space to be near, or within easy reach, of the Lower School.

51. Finally, the rooms on the entrance level Block A, at present used for careers guidance and clubs, are converted into a community suite. It includes provision for careers guidance, interviews with parents, parent/teachers association meetings, discussions and talks. This accommodation is carpeted and has shelving or display boarding on all walls, with coffee tables and low seating for informal conversation and working-height chairs and tables for study, reading or writing.

Summary of Modifications to the English Model (see Figure 4 and Table 5)

52. In the light of the foregoing adjustments, the following decisions, summarised in note form, were made:

   i) No attempt should be made to adapt any of the existing building for indoor physical education. It is assumed that the Ministry of Youth and Sports will eventually provide either a gymnasium or sports hall (or both) for the use of the school and community. Outdoor physical education facilities already exist.

   ii) Accept the existing dining and kitchen arrangements but re-furnish the dining area.

Figure 4

Revised Model for Sucy-en-Brie

This figure shows the organisation of the pedagogical model revised from that shown in Figure 1 and reflecting the decisions taken and modifications made to the English model.

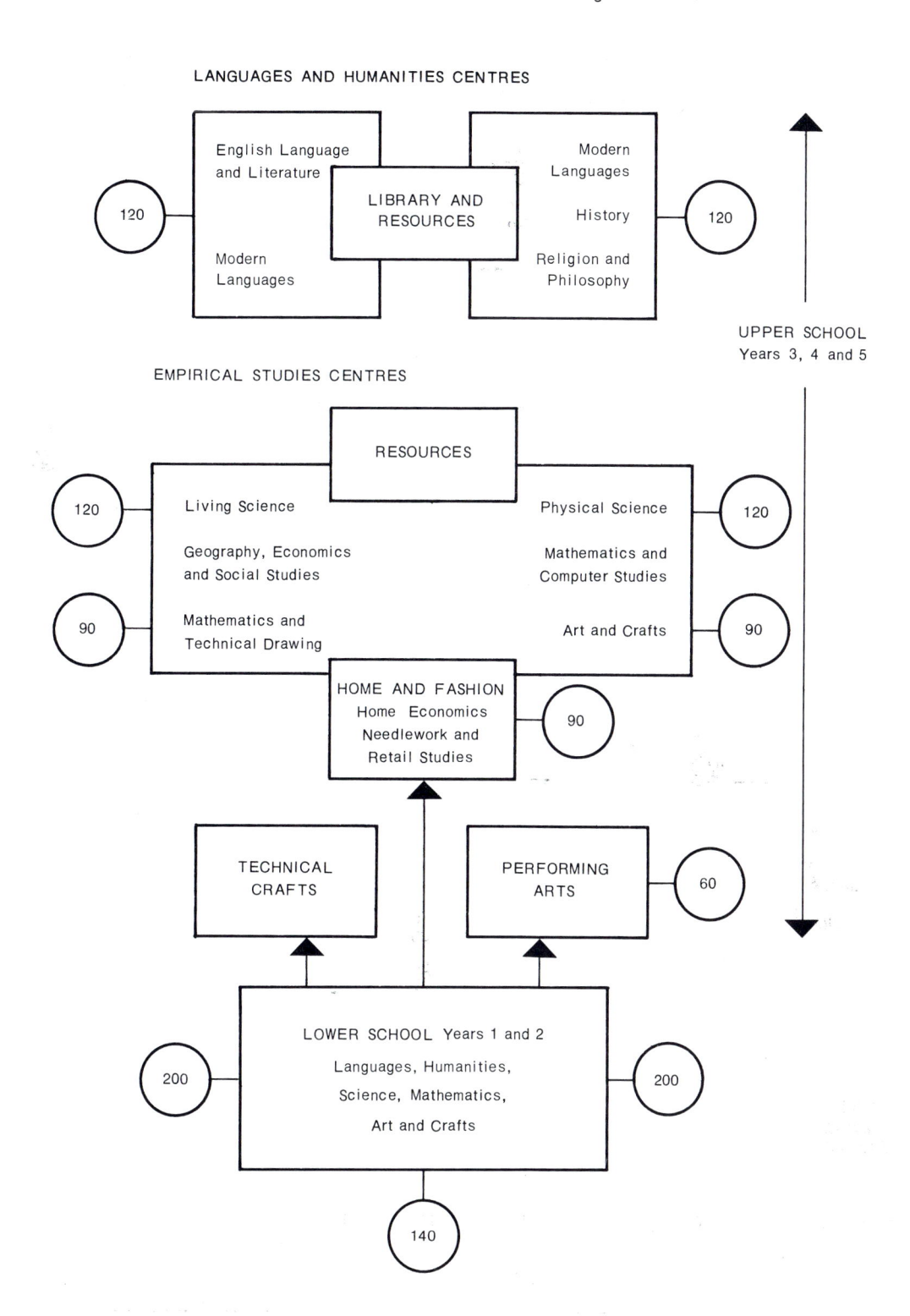

LANGUAGES AND HUMANITIES CENTRES

- English Language and Literature
- Modern Languages
- LIBRARY AND RESOURCES
- Modern Languages
- History
- Religion and Philosophy

120 — 120

UPPER SCHOOL Years 3, 4 and 5

EMPIRICAL STUDIES CENTRES

RESOURCES

- Living Science
- Geography, Economics and Social Studies
- Mathematics and Technical Drawing
- Physical Science
- Mathematics and Computer Studies
- Art and Crafts

120 — 120
90 — 90

HOME AND FASHION
Home Economics
Needlework and
Retail Studies

90

TECHNICAL CRAFTS

PERFORMING ARTS

60

LOWER SCHOOL Years 1 and 2
Languages, Humanities, Science, Mathematics, Art and Crafts

200 — 200

140

iii) Accept the location of the existing administrative offices and make only minor modifications.
iv) Retain that area of the garage not used for the drama studio.
v) Re-design the technical workshop block to provide four workshop areas plus a large storage space.
vi) Lower School
— to be accommodated mainly at basement level but also to include Block B at ground level;
— to have immediate access to the outside which is of great advantage to the youngest pupils;
— to retain its own lavatory and cloakroom area;
— each of the three platforms to provide the base for a social group of the Lower School.
vii) Humanities Departments
— humanities I and II to be accommodated in adjoining Blocks C and D at second floor level and physically linked by a substantial library and resource area.
viii) Empirical Studies Departments
— each of the empirical studies departments is too large to be accommodated in two adjoining platforms; hence a fifth platform should be incorporated to form a related department of home and fashion studies.
ix) Performing Arts
— located in Block C at ground level, to include a large music studio for orchestral work and a music teaching room, a large drama workshop and a classroom for English literature.
x) Social Structure of the School and Community Bases. Departments should incorporate the following social bases:
Lower School—3 bases for 200, 200 and 140 pupils respectively.
Upper School—based in eight groups as follows:

Humanities I	120
Humanities II	120
Empirical Studies I	120 and 90
Empirical Studies II	120 and 90
Home and Fashion Studies	90
Performing Arts	60

Table 5
Sucy-en-Brie. Revised Distribution of Workplaces and Social Places.

In the following table, the distribution of workplaces and social places is amended from that shown in Table 3 to reflect the decisions taken and modifications made to the English model.

	Humanities I	Humanities II	Empirical Studies I	Empirical Studies II	Home and Fashion	Performing Arts	Physical Education	Technical Centre	Lower School
English	90					25			70
Modern Languages	36	35							40
History		45							30
Religion and Philosophy		45							30
Geography, etc.			67						44
Mathematics			85	30					70
Science			54	79					60
Art and Crafts				90					36
Needlework					44				
Home Economics					66				
Music						75			
Drama						42			
Wood and Metalwork								88	
Technical Drawing			22						
Physical Education							68 indoor 68 outdoor		
Library, Resources and Study	30	30	15	15	10	10			30
Social Places	120	120	120 90	120 90	90	60			200 200 140

Area Summary

53. As a result of the decisions made, the floor areas given over to the various departments are as follows:

Lower School	(a)+(a)+(b)	1,711.218m^2
Humanities I	(a)	622.430m^2
Humanities II	(a)	622.430m^2
Empirical Studies I	(a)+(b)	1,088.788m^2
Empirical Studies II	(a)+(b)	1,088.788m^2
Home and Fashion Studies	(a)	622.430m^2
Performing Arts	(a)	622.430m^2
Technical Centre		515.595m^2
Administration	(b)	466.358m^2
Dining and Kitchen	(a)	622.439m^2
		7,982.897m^2

Minimum teaching area (MTA) requirement = 5,173.601m^2
= 64.8% of the total floor area

The Solution (Plans 11 to 14 inclusive)

54. In the design of English schools, emphasis is placed on the quality of the environmental conditions. Whereas in Sucy-en-Brie there is a great degree of uniformity of character throughout the teaching space, English schools are characterised by their variety, spaces differing from each other according to the nature of the activities followed and the quality of the human relationships established within them. Hence, re-design which merely shows a re-arrangement of partition walls and a re-furnishing of the spaces provides an incomplete picture of adaptation to meet the requirements of the English model. The adapted building should also match the variety and quality of the environmental conditions to be found in an English school.

55. Space relationships are at two levels: first, between the various departments—this tends to become less important as departments become inter-disciplinary; and second within the departments themselves—these are the relationships between teaching spaces designed for particular activities, study and resource areas and social spaces.

56. The actual design process for each of the departments was remarkably similar despite the differing departmental functions. Once the overall decisions had been made as to which department was to go where, the detailed planning tended to follow these steps:

   i) discussing possible sequences of learning activities within the department to determine the relationship to each other of the different types of workplaces;
   ii) considering zones of learning activity ranging from those which are essentially quiet and sedate to those in which a high degree of physical movement might be involved;
   iii) accommodating basic class groups of 24 to 30 pupils while at the same time allowing for considerable variation in group organisation;
   iv) deciding which spaces need to be closed for uninterrupted supervised work and which need partial enclosures only so as to give any access to the open, active working areas being designed;
   v) considering the articulation of the open work areas and social spaces by mobile furniture and storage units so as to give maximum advantage to the work and social life of the department;
   vi) assessing the services required by special learning activities (e.g. science, crafts, drama) and to locate such workplaces where they can be most economically provided, using existing services to the full;
   vii) assessing the scale of storage required and using existing provision wherever possible;
   viii) providing the clothes hanging space required by the community based in the department;
   ix) providing the teaching staff facilities (departmental staff centre, tutor rooms and offices) most helpful to the organisation of the department.

57. A first main problem in this adaptation, therefore, was the fitting of the departments of the English model into the existing Sucy-en-Brie building units. Adaptability clearly varies according to the form of the building and the floor areas available in the building units. Linear forms, though presenting fewer physical problems in terms of lighting and ventilation, do not make possible effective groupings of inter-related spaces so essential to the workings of a department. On the other hand, extensive square and rectangular forms, which offer the simplest geometrical solutions to space and departmental relationships, depreciate the quality of life in schools and are coming to be regarded as alien to its objectives and aspirations. Complicated routes through them are often a disturbing factor in the working of a school. Sucy-en-Brie afforded distinct advantages in the sizes of its platforms and in their relation to one another.

Plan 11 : SUCY-EN-BRIE ENGLISH MODEL BASEMENT LEVEL

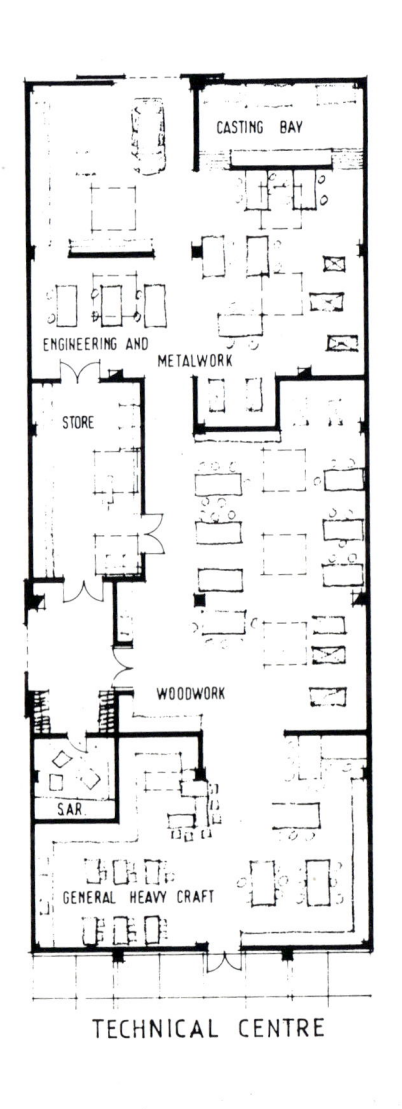

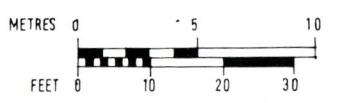

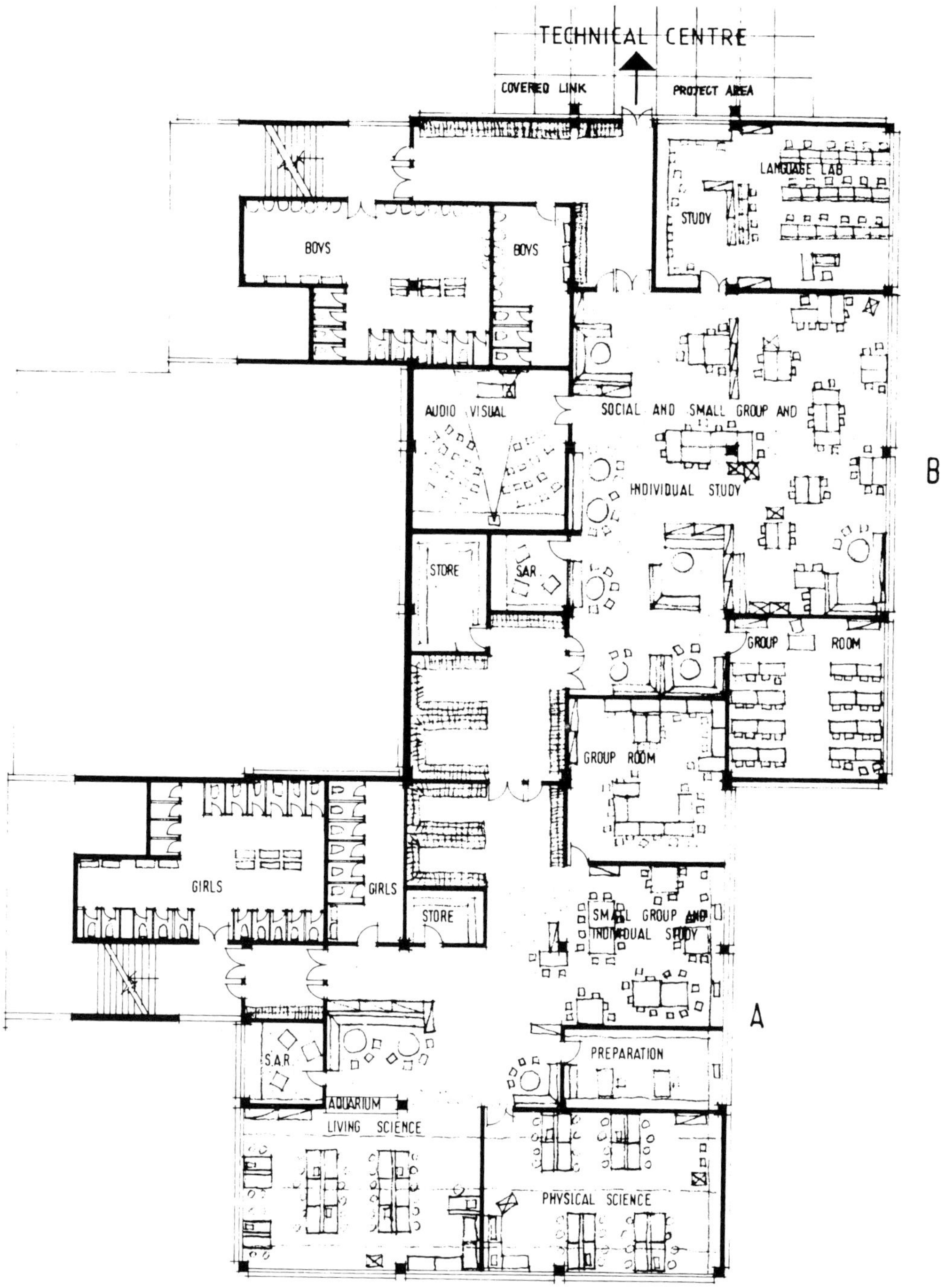
TECHNICAL CENTRE
COVERED LINK
PROJECT AREA
LANGUAGE LAB
STUDY
BOYS
BOYS
AUDIO VISUAL
SOCIAL AND SMALL GROUP AND
INDIVIDUAL STUDY
B
STORE
SAR
GROUP ROOM
GROUP ROOM
GIRLS
GIRLS
STORE
SMALL GROUP AND
INDIVIDUAL STUDY
A
SAR
PREPARATION
AQUARIUM
LIVING SCIENCE
PHYSICAL SCIENCE

Plan 12 : SUCY-EN-BRIE ENGLISH MODEL ENTRANCE LEVEL

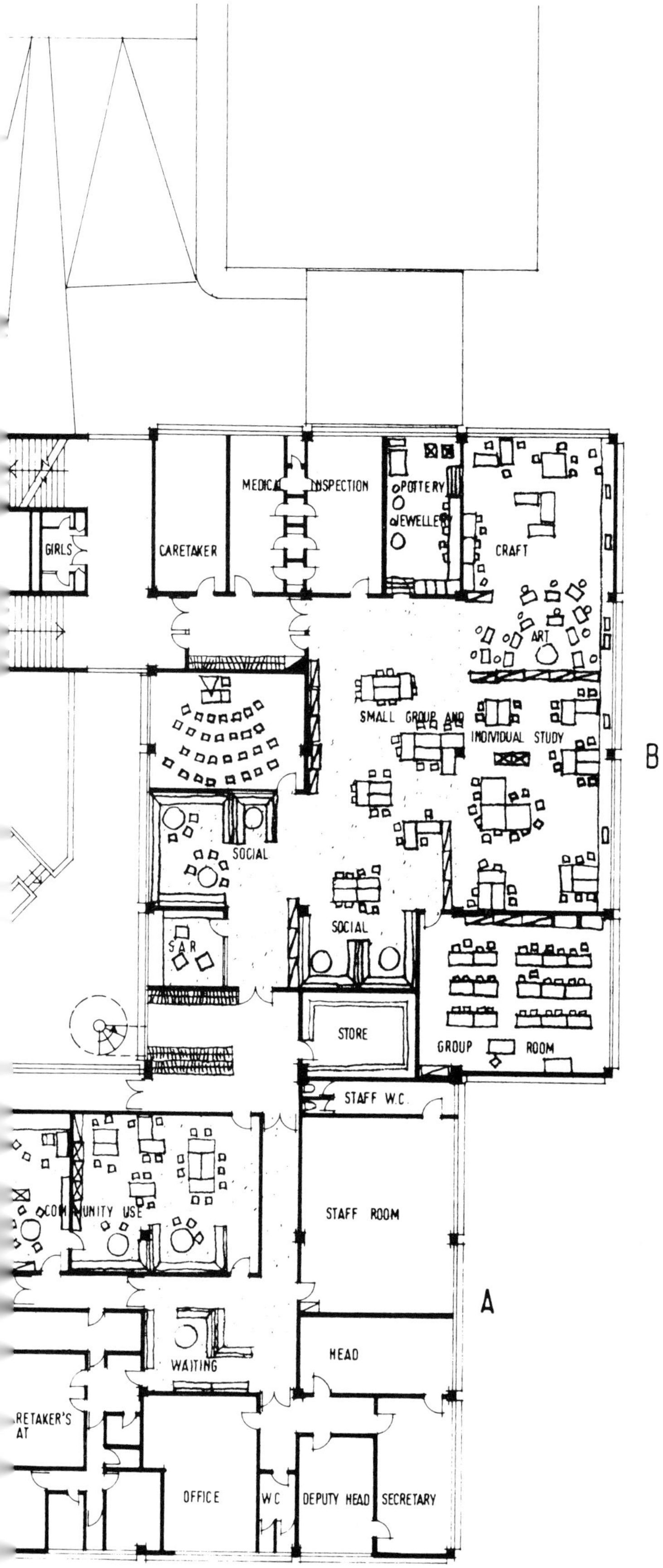
MEDICAL INSPECTION
POTTERY
JEWELLERY
CRAFT
GIRLS
CARETAKER
ART
SMALL GROUP AND INDIVIDUAL STUDY
B
SOCIAL
SOCIAL
S.A.R
STORE
GROUP ROOM
STAFF W.C.
COMMUNITY USE
STAFF ROOM
A
WAITING
HEAD
RETAKER'S
AT
OFFICE
W.C
DEPUTY HEAD
SECRETARY

Plan 13 : SUCY-EN-BRIE ENGLISH MODEL FIRST FLOOR LEVEL

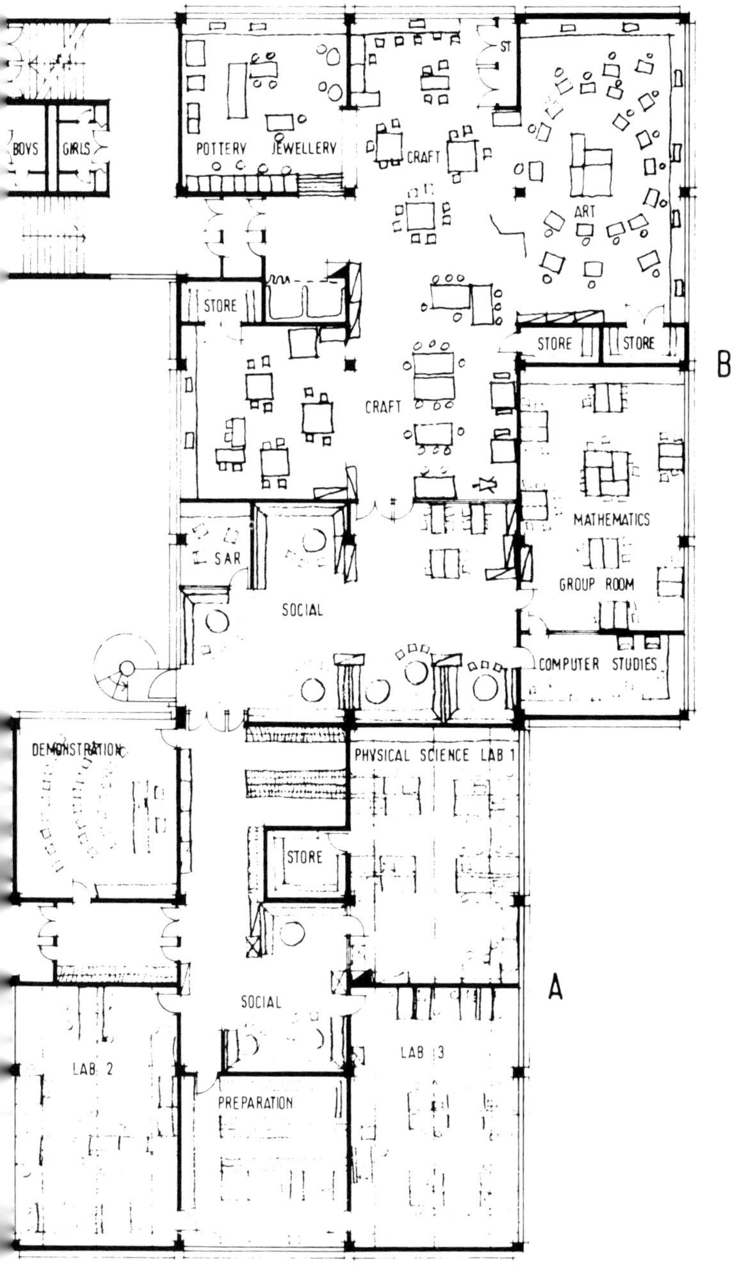
BOYS
GIRLS
POTTERY
JEWELLERY
CRAFT
ST
ART
STORE
STORE
STORE
CRAFT
B
MATHEMATICS
GROUP ROOM
SAR
SOCIAL
COMPUTER STUDIES
DEMONSTRATION
PHYSICAL SCIENCE LAB 1
STORE
A
SOCIAL
LAB 2
LAB 3
PREPARATION

Plan 14 : **SUCY-EN-BRIE ENGLISH MODEL SECOND FLOOR LEVEL**

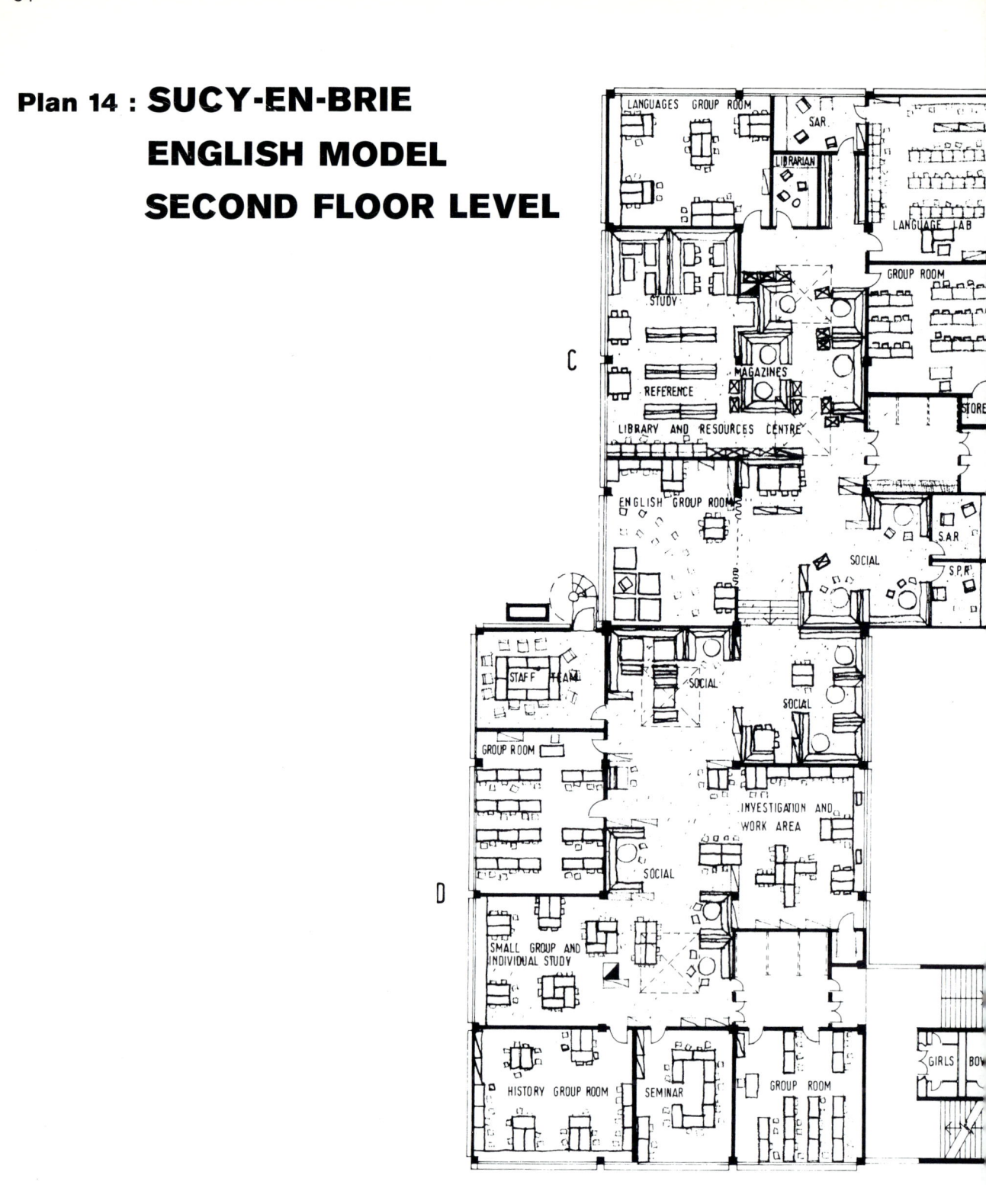

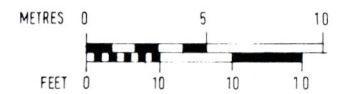

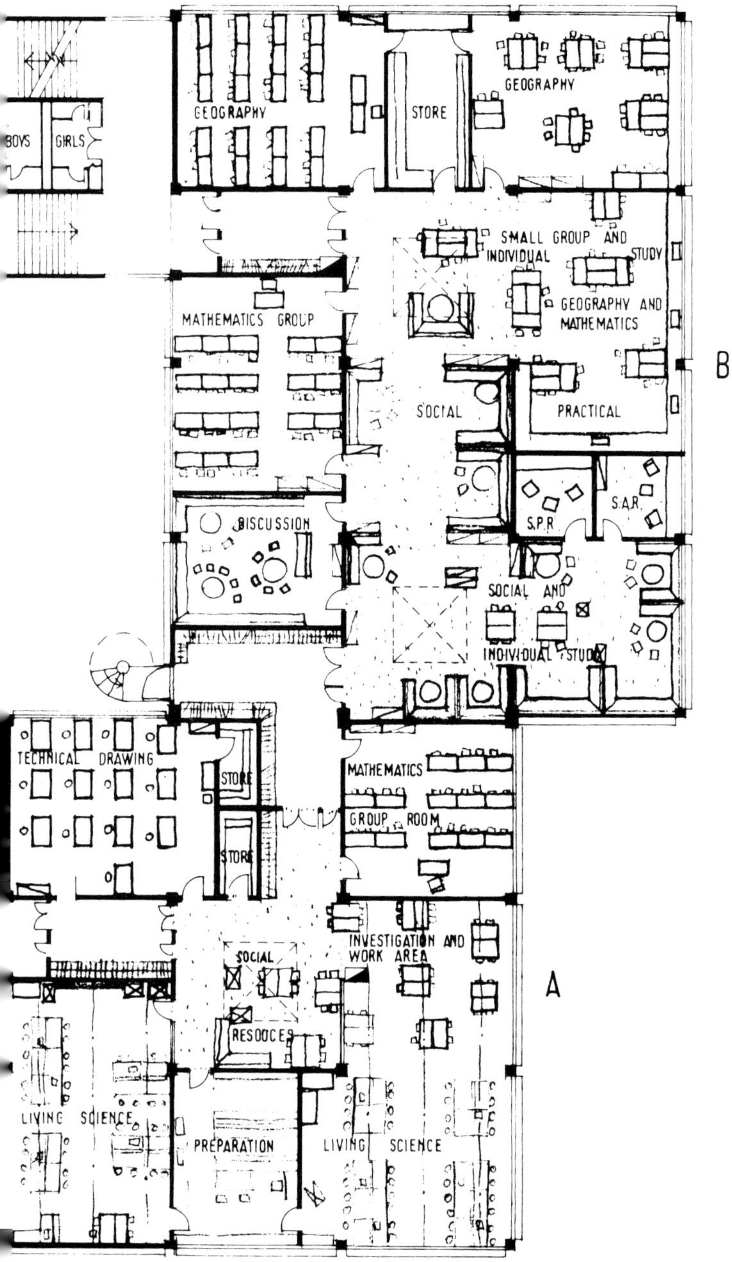
GEOGRAPHY
STORE
GEOGRAPHY
BOYS
GIRLS
SMALL GROUP AND INDIVIDUAL STUDY
GEOGRAPHY AND MATHEMATICS
MATHEMATICS GROUP
SOCIAL
PRACTICAL
B
DISCUSSION
S.P.R.
S.A.R.
SOCIAL AND INDIVIDUAL STUDY
TECHNICAL DRAWING
STORE
STORE
MATHEMATICS GROUP ROOM
INVESTIGATION AND WORK AREA
SOCIAL
RESOUCES
A
LIVING SCIENCE
PREPARATION
LIVING SCIENCE

58. In order to make the most productive use of "dead" circulation areas in the centres of the platforms, it was important to take down some internal partitions so as to let in daylight and give the users the visual comfort of at least long window views to the outside. Such space then became usable as social or resources accommodation as well as circulation space. Hence the width of blocks is eventually determined by light penetration. A major problem was how can a central area topped up with artificial lighting be not only tolerable but stimulating? Enclosed spaces with an artificially controlled environment should be used for short periods only and it can be asked do such spaces earn their keep?

59. For cost reasons it was expedient to leave partition walls in their present position wherever possible. It proved difficult to get a variety of rooms of suitable shape, each with some daylight. There was a lack of small rooms particularly to serve as departmental H.Q., tutorial rooms or offices for teachers with special responsibility. Sucy-en-Brie was quite unadaptable in terms of physical education and difficult in terms of drama. It might be profitable to carry out an exercise in gutting one platform of all partition walls and re-designing the area to accommodate a department. The "best" could then be compared with the "good" and a judgement made whether it was worth the extra cost.

60. An English school demands normal services (water, drainage, gas, electricity) almost everywhere. All departments have easy access to W.C. and washing accommodation. Water is available in most working areas as most subjects have a field of practical work for which it is needed (the universal sink). Hence the platforms lacking such services were much less adaptable than those which had them and it had to be assumed that a minimum of such services would be provided. The heaviest demand will probably be in the new "home and fashion" department located in a platform which is at present lacking in essential services.

61. The more open design of platforms, together with a facile use of furniture, have achieved teaching arrangements which, though acceptable today, would not have been so a few years ago. Moreover, they would not now be acceptable in many European countries. Nevertheless, successful adaptation depends upon substantial acoustic treatment of the interior to make working arrangements in these more open conditions tolerable. This would include the carpeting of extensive areas, especially those through which circulation is necessary, and those which require an environmental character conducive to quiet conversation, study or tutoring. If the money necessary is not spent at the outset, then the open conditions are quite likely to be totally intolerable.

62. The problems of designing a secondary school for pupils of 11 to 16 years of age are relatively simple as compared with those of a secondary school with a substantial sixth form (students of 16 to 18 years of age). A much more highly articulated building is required for the latter, providing as it must for teaching groups of say 3 to 15 students, much of whose work is necessarily conducted in closed spaces. A large number of tutor rooms and offices would therefore be required. To have adapted Sucy-en-Brie for a school of 1,200 (11 to 16 pupils)+200 (16 to 18 students) would have been a very difficult task. Sucy-en-Brie was never designed in the first place with the needs of older students in mind, and it would perhaps have been quite unreasonable to make such demands of its accommodation.

63. The design of social space needs special consideration. It serves mainly as the home-base for a community of the school and the informal association of its members. But it also makes an important contribution to the actual educational programme of the school and is often accountable as teaching space within the area requirements of English Building Regulations. For teaching purposes, it may provide for private study, both formal and informal, for group discussions, for the briefing of project groups and even for more formal seminars. It is, in fact, most productively used when related to group investigation and project spaces in patterns of resource based education. Where there is good acoustic treatment of the environment and where mobile furniture and storage units facilitate change in the physical arrangements, there is little conflict between the social and teaching requirements of the space. The design of more flexible teaching arrangements, combined with the revolutionary changes in school furniture, have almost removed any differences of character and environment which existed between social and teaching space.

Degrees of Adaptability

64. The following summarises the qualities of the Sucy-en-Brie school in meeting the changes which the English model school demanded:

Adaptable features

i) The suitability of the platforms (in both shape and size) for accommodating the departments of the English school.
ii) Light penetration within the platforms which facilitates the application of "DES Guidelines on Environmental Conditions" to the building.
iii) The external staircases which allowed all the space on the platforms to be usable in re-design. Seldom did it impose circulation routes through them.
iv) The ability to add, replace or remove internal partitions independently of the structure of the building.

Unadaptable features

i) The limited spread of essential services. In an English school:
— sanitary and washing facilities are provided in each department;
— water power supplies are available in each department.
ii) The lack of satisfactory acoustic control throughout the building to enable floor space to be opened up for re-arrangement of the activity areas.
iii) Wall and floor finishes unsympathetic to the requirement for variety in the character of activity areas e.g.
— quiet areas for discussion, tutoring and study;
— the special character of social areas in encouraging association without generating undue noise and disturbance;
— reducing the sound of movement in learning areas where movement is necessary to the activity.
iv) The difficulty of creating large spaces for drama, ballet and dancing without intruding pillar. (It is accepted that the school is not designed for indoor physical education—gymnastics, games and athletic practice.)

Table 6
Area Analysis of Sucy-en-Brie as Existing
(Excluding Caretaker's Flat, Cycle Garage, Covered Links).

	Basement Level	Entrance Level	First Floor Level	Second Floor Level	Total	Percentage
Teaching	800.64	508.64	1,114.56	1,607.04	4,030.88	45.81
Ancillary	444.60	172.00	263.92	99.76	980.28	11.41
Administration	79.92	421.14			501.06	5.69
Circulation	513.60	522.78	641.28	857.28	2,534.94	28.81
Dining			311.04		311.04	3.54
Kitchen		140.04	233.28		373.32	4.24
Boilers, Plant		68.04			68.04	0.77
Total	1,838.76	1,832.64	2,564.08	2,564.08	8,799.60	100.00

Table 7
Area Analysis of Sucy-en-Brie English Model
(Excluding Caretaker's Flat, Cycle Garage, Covered Links).

	Basement Level	Entrance Level	First Floor Level	Second Floor Level	Total	Percentage
Teaching	1,171.44	1.086.12	1,481.76	1,900.16	5,639.48	61.28
Ancillary	284.76	154.84	132.88	152.32	724.80	7.88
Administration	38.88	288.00	28.08	39.96	394.92	4.29
Circulation	343.68	499.08	377.04	471.64	1,691.44	18.38
Dining			311.04		311.04	3.38
Kitchen		140.04	233.28		373.32	4.06
Boilers, Plant		68.04			68.04	0.73
Total	1,838.76	2,236.12	2,564.08	2,564.08	9,203.04	100.00

ARLINGTON

The School as Existing
(Plans 15 to 17 inclusive)

65. The Arlington Senior Public School, Borough of York, Canada, was built in 1970-71 for about 700 pupils aged 12 to 14 years. It is a rectangular, three-storey building with four external stair towers connecting all floors. Main extrance is at the middle floor level, giving direct access to the administrative offices. On this same floor is the technical teaching accommodation comprising departments for visual and industrial arts, home economics and general science. At basement level is the dining accommodation which also serves as a drama and assembly space for the school, the music department and two gymnasia with adjoining changing and shower facilities. The main teaching accommodation is at first-floor level, with a large central library and resources area, flanked by learning and social space, much of which is of an open or fluid nature. Articulation of these learning areas is by specially designed mobile furniture and storage units. The four common room spaces and associated learning areas reflect the four-house system on the basis of which the school is organised. Each "house" has a membership of 165 to 200 pupils of mixed ages and academic ability, drawn from many contributory schools. The object of the house system is to give each pupil a sense of security and individuality within the framework of a large school. A "house" has its own team of five or six teachers, each of whom is a home teacher to a class group and responsible for their pastoral care, as in a primary school. Some features of the organisation are, in fact, not unlike those of an English school and reflect the movement from a mass education system towards one concerned with individual development.

66. The school building was designed to cope with future changes, firstly in the open character of some of its learning areas and secondly in its furniture and equipment which enabled it to respond to evolutionary change. Its relocatable partitions intend to assist this process. The school would like to have enclosed more spaces for small group work but this is dependent upon generous scales of staffing. During periods of economic stringency when fewer teachers tend to be employed, open and fluid space arrangements assist in the supervision of several working groups by a single teacher, provided the environmental conditions favour such mobility. Space standards in this Canadian school are much more generous than in comparable English or French secondary schools. With a total floor area of 7,351m^2 offering 10.50m^2 per pupil. the Arlington school has ample space in which to operate.

67. The building is a three-storey rectangular block 30.480m wide by 83.820m long, sub-divided on a 1.524m × 1.524m grid and linked vertically by two external stair towers on each of the long sides. The reinforced concrete frame gives spans up to 15.240m increasing to 30.480m clear in the gymnasium.[1] External cladding is by pre-cast concrete units or window units based on the grid, except for the stair towers which are clad in in situ bush-hammered concrete. Internal walls that are fire resistant or around blocks of lavatory accommodation are masonry. Elsewhere relocatable partitions are used of three types: fully glazed; glazed above a 1.067m sill; and solid. After the first year of use of the school, two partitions were relocated and more constructed to enclose two areas that had initially been only partly enclosed. Although the school would have liked to enclose more spaces for smaller group activities, they were restricted by a reduction in the teaching staff to 33 full-time teachers in the 1973-74 academic year. All services run through the ceiling void on the 5 foot × 5 foot (1.524m × 1.524m) grid such that they can be "plugged-into" as necessary virtually anywhere in the teaching areas.

Fitting the Model into the Building

Area considerations

68. Using the same English model as at Sucy-en-Brie, a secondary school for 1,350 students of 11 to 16 years needs approximately 9,200m^2 of floor area i.e. 6.5m^2 per pupil plus a small margin for wastage in adapting an existing building. This is roughly the floor area used at Sucy-en-Brie. The floor area available at Arlington is roughly 7,100m^2 so that 2,100m^2 of new building would be needed to meet the

---

1. The school, and the system in which it is built, were designed to imperial measurements; thus the block is 100 feet wide × 275 feet long, sub-divided on a 5 foot × 5 foot grid; the frame gives spans of up to 50 feet increasing to 100 feet clear in the gymnasium.

requirements of the English model. The following courses of action were considered:

i) to write a new model for a smaller comprehensive school; this however would lessen the comparative nature of the exercise with that done on Sucy-en-Brie;

ii) to convert the gymnasium and first floor void into teaching area by constructing a floor across the void and altering the changing accommodation to teaching area; but this would not represent good value for money (i.e. changing the function of expensive specialist accommodation); as at Sucy-en-Brie, the best use should be made of those facilities provided;

iii) to add another floor to the building or investigate other means of extending the floor area by additions; this might, however, lead to unreasonable disruption of the school; it might also not be feasible to extend the building vertically and the site appears to be too restricted to extend horizontally;

iv) to assume that the district needs a secondary school for 1,350 pupils; accept the building as it stands and add some new building; (as was done in the Sucy-en-Brie exercise where it was assumed that physical education provision would be made elsewhere in the locality); this is the most expedient solution and offers the best comparison with Sucy-en-Brie, but depends on an exercise being done to determine which part of the school would be best housed elsewhere as a viable unit.

69. Having decided to adopt a solution as in *iv)* above, it was then necessary to determine which departments could function successfully on a site elsewhere. Any decision to locate particular specialist departments and social communities of the school on a site at some distance from the parent building would depend upon the numbers of students and teachers involved in movement between the two buildings, and the ability of the isolated communities to lead a partly independent life. Departments used by the whole school would involve all pupils moving from one building to the other. Any Upper School department so situated would involve all the Upper School in the movement. It became clear that greatest advantage lay in locating the Lower School elsewhere for three main reasons:

i) The Lower School requires minimal use of specialist space and facilities. A Lower School building might be so designed that pupils need go to the main building for physical education and technical crafts only, not more than 20 per cent of their programme. They would also dine there. The Lower School would need to have its own library and resource facilities, though they would be subsidiary to those in the Upper School.

ii) The Lower School can operate as a cohesive unit socially and create a semi-independent life for its pupils.

iii) 2,100m^2 of floor space should amply provide for its needs.

The Arlington site is too restricted to allow of further new building within it. Hence, a separate nearby site would have to be found for the new Lower School building.

Physical constraints

70. The decision to adapt the existing Arlington building for the use of the Upper School and for such special facilities as are shared with the Lower School (physical education facilities, the technical craft spaces and the dining accommodation) is in accord with the broad requirements of the English model and no major modification to the brief is needed. The deep rectangular form of the Arlington building imposes physical constraints on the design of the various departments however. Circulation areas are far more generous than is standard in English schools and to fit the teaching area required into the building some of the corridor areas must be taken over for teaching purposes. The positioning of the stair towers and the toilet areas together effectively blank off a large proportion of available window wall; this makes it virtually impossible to give every teaching space adequate daylight to meet the DES environmental guidelines. Likewise, the deep plan would appear to cause great difficulties in securing an outside view from every teaching area. However, due to the building system used it should be possible to increase the amount of glazing by replacing precast concrete panels by window panels.

71. The width of the block (30.480m), when split by the necessary linear circulation along its length (83.820m), produces difficult widths which are not easily sub-divided into the areas needed for teaching groups of 30 or the practical areas characteristic of English school design. It might prove more economical if the main circulation route were not centrally oriented along the length of the block—even if this meant an increase in circulation space due to duplication on either side of a central band of accommodation (this band to be employed for storage, audio-visual rooms, dark rooms and other areas not continuously used).

Plan 15 : **ARLINGTON AS EXISTING**

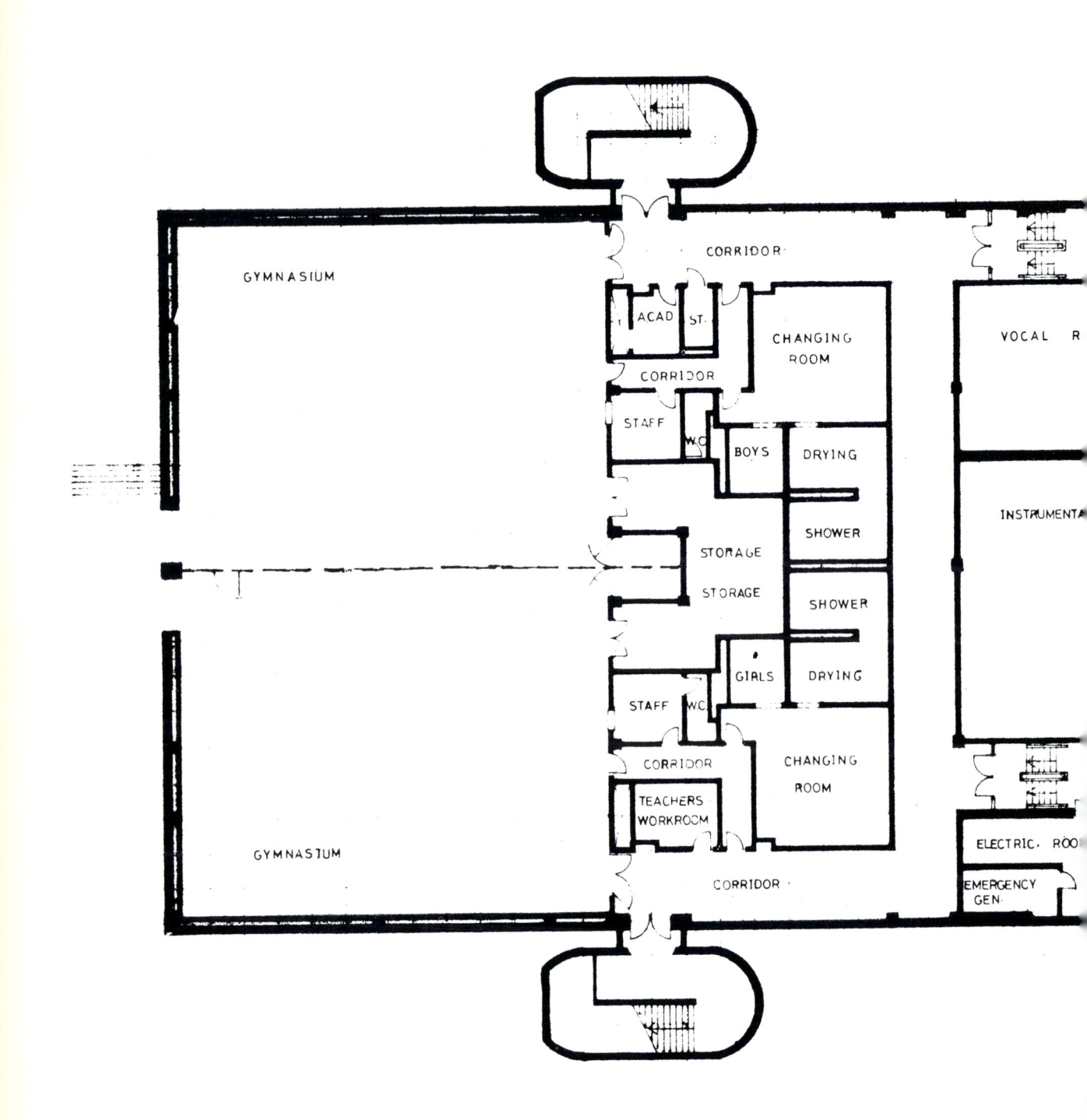

BASEMENT LEVEL

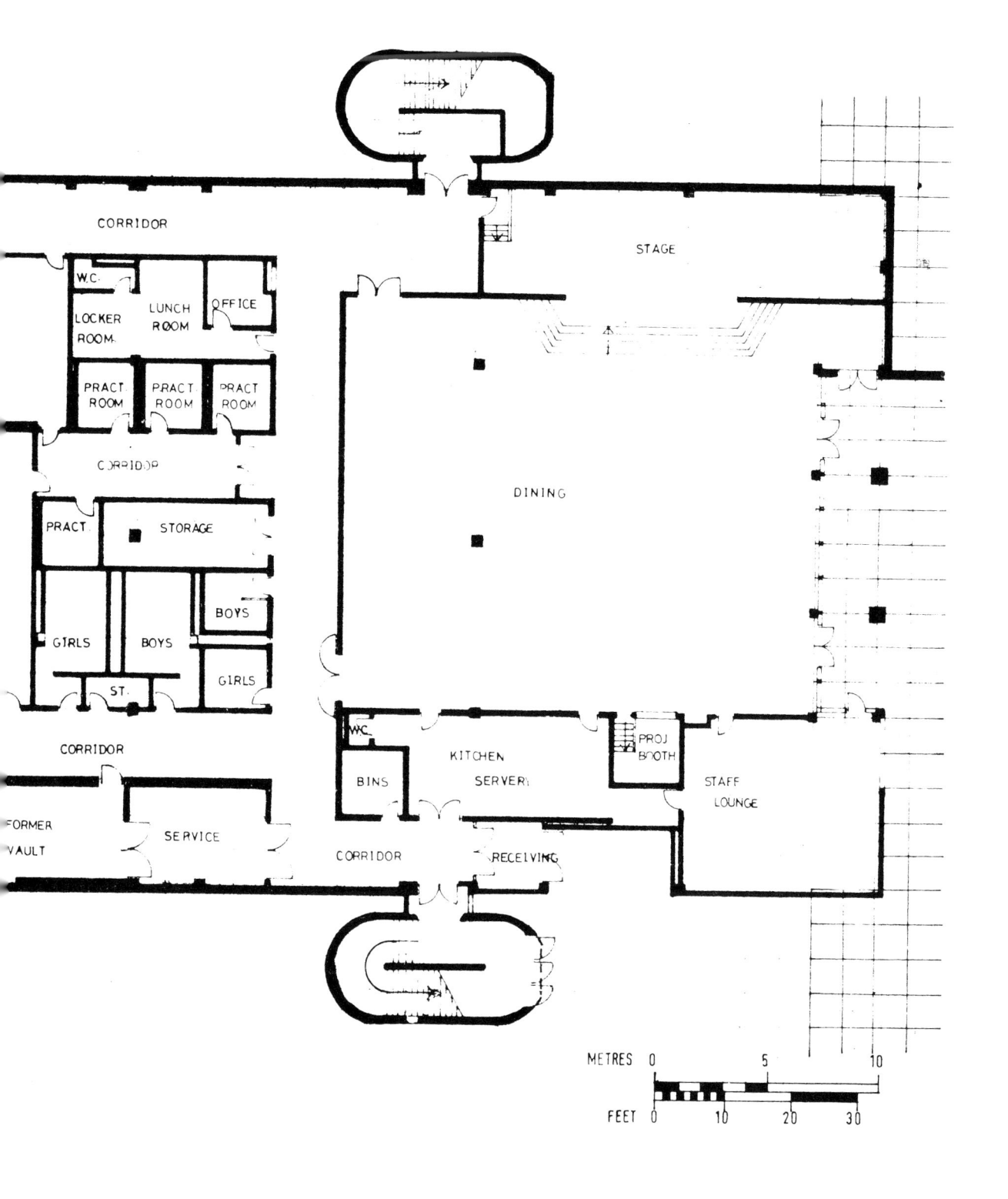

Plan 16 : **ARLINGTON AS EXISTING**

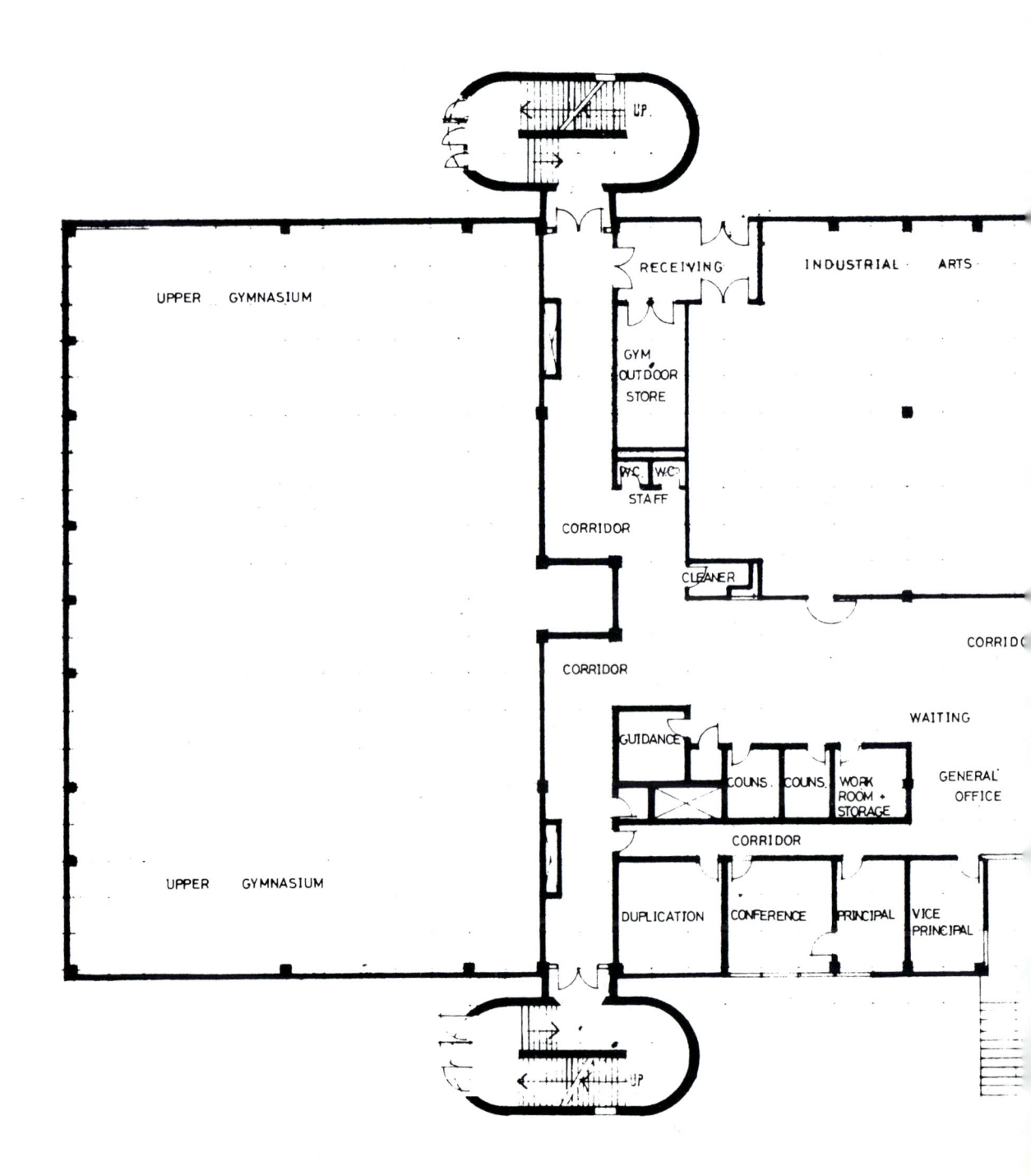

ENTRANCE LEVEL

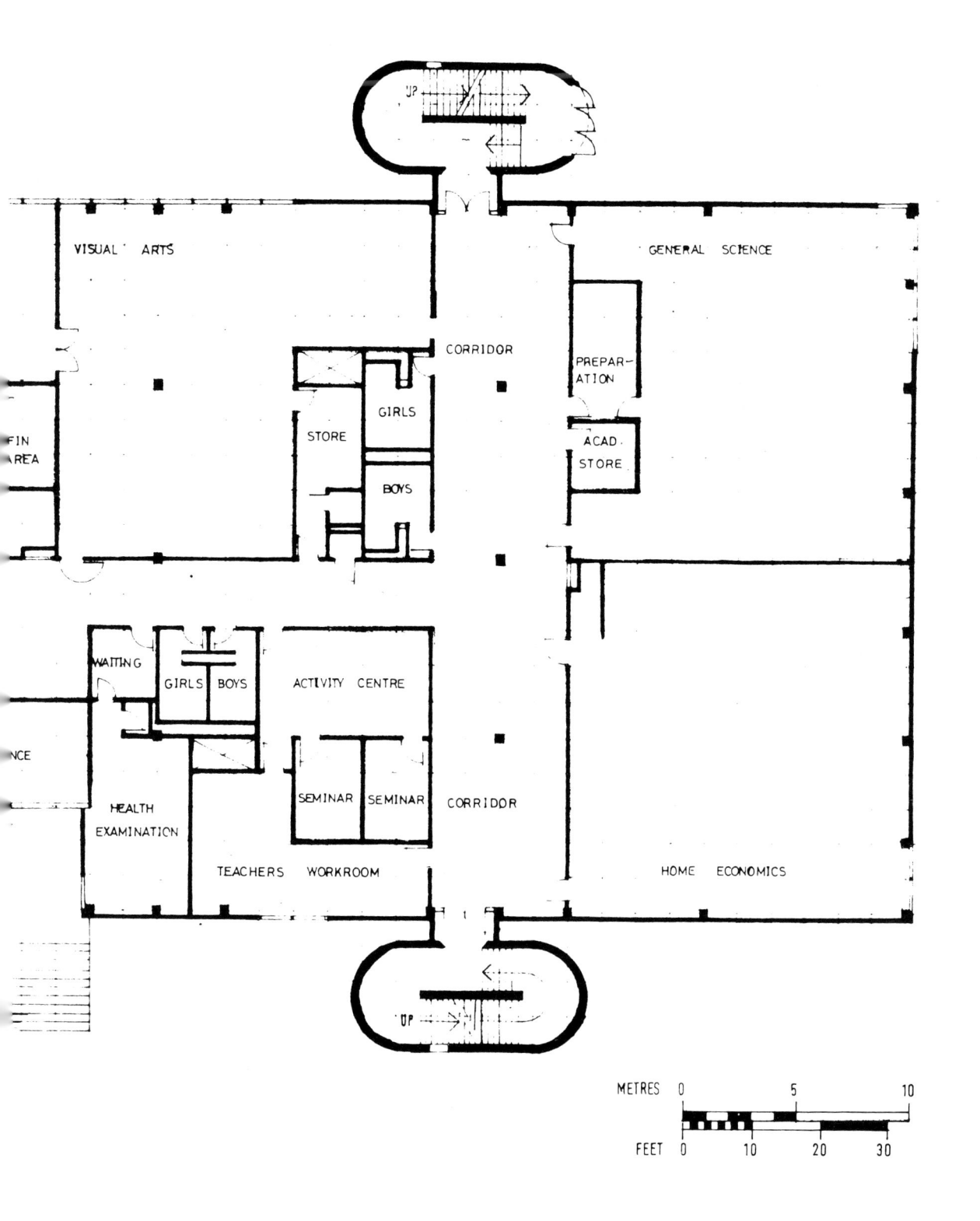

64

Plan 17 : **ARLINGTON AS EXISTING**

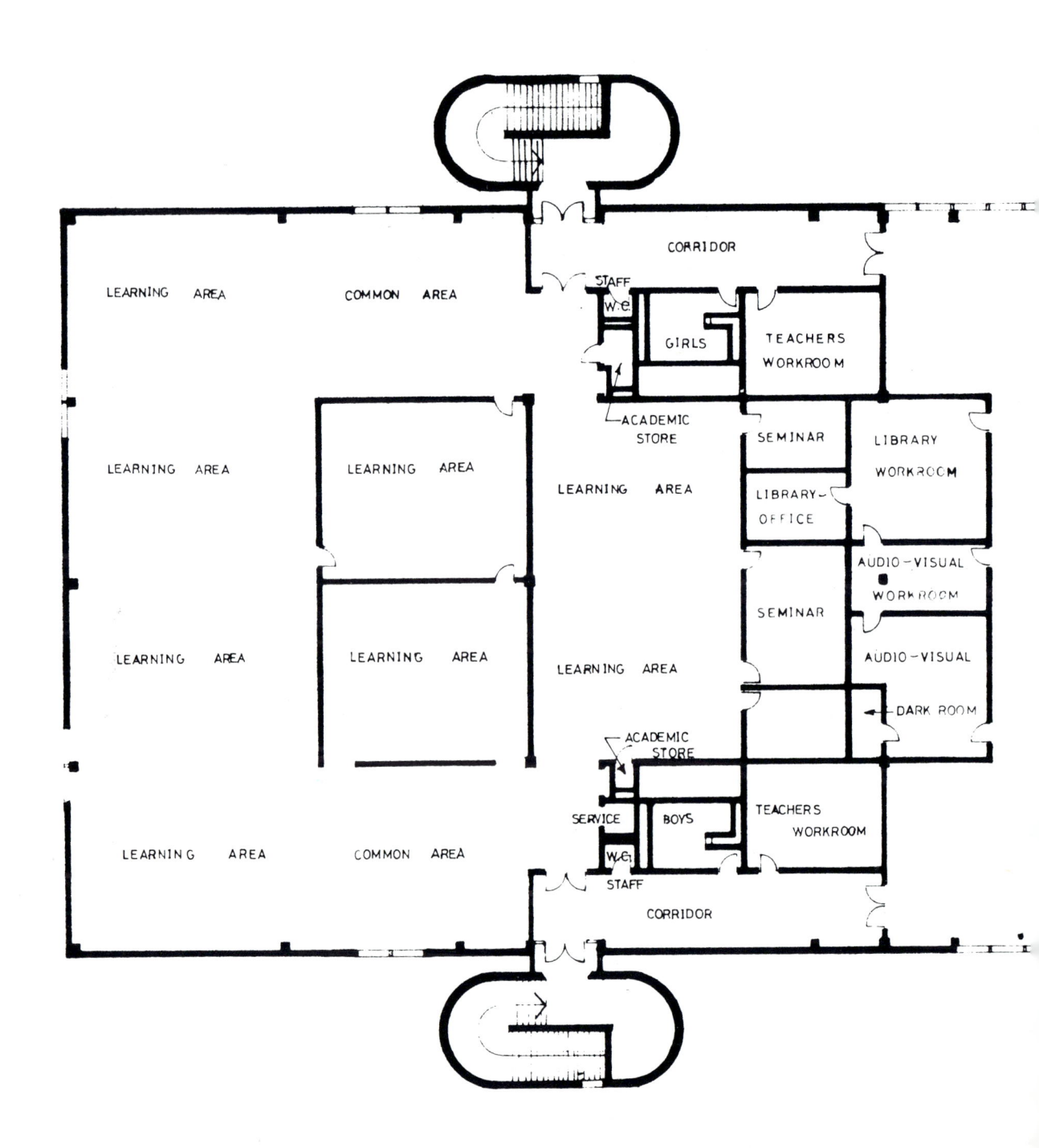

FIRST FLOOR LEVEL

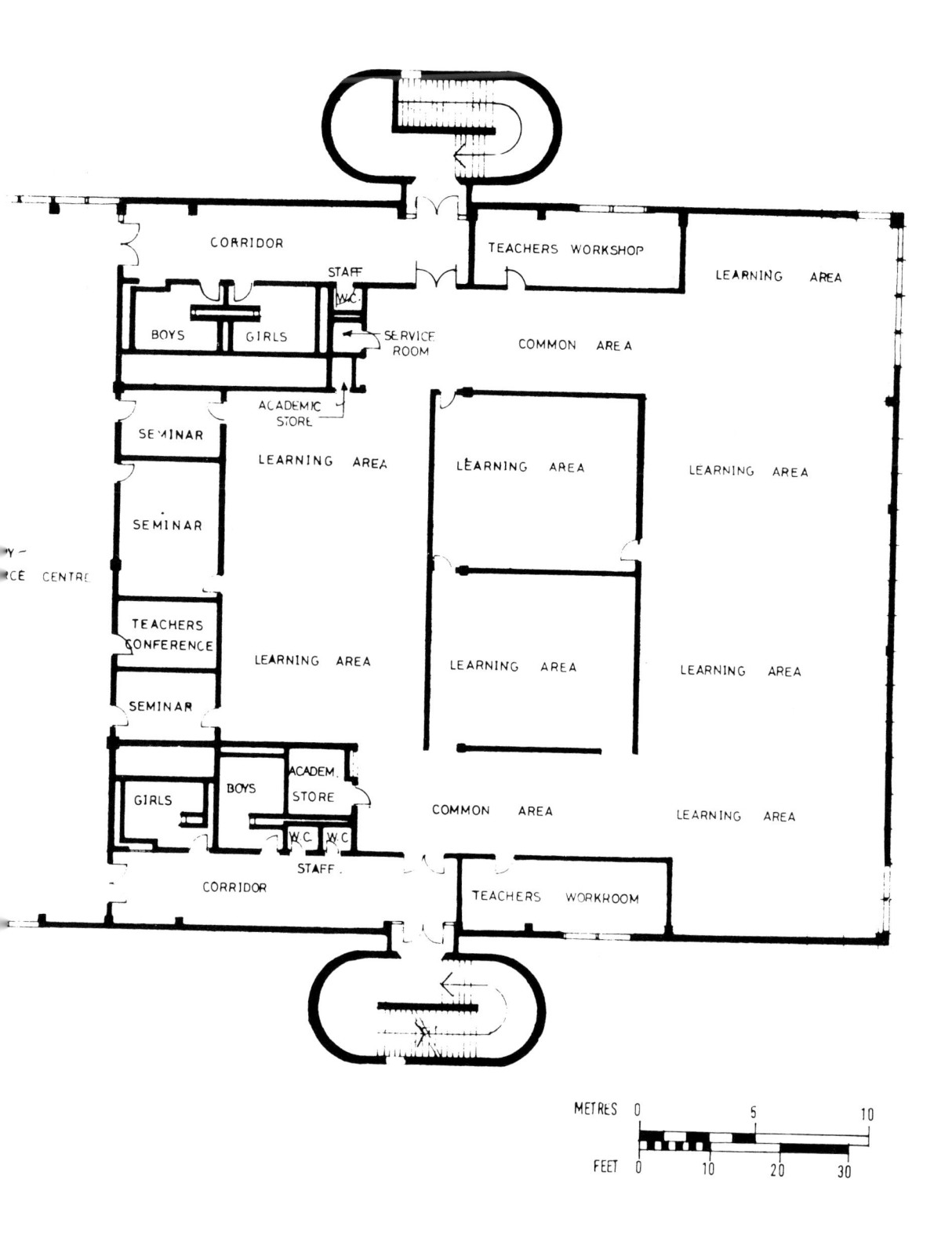

65

A rough calculation of the approximate number of perimeter teaching areas required is twenty-two needing approximately 201 linear metres. The useful available length is approximately 146 linear metres. This means that about 25 per cent of the teaching areas must be accommodated at the centre of the plan. If possible, these teaching areas should be of the type in which the students are unlikely to spend long periods.

72. To meet DES standards for toilet accommodation it is necessary to provide two fittings per 30 students. Taking the situation in which the building would be at maximum occupancy (when 30 per cent of the Lower School students would be in the building along with all the Upper School students—30 per cent of 540 plus 810), 65 fittings are required. In the existing building only 38 fittings are provided. Although some adaptations can be made within the existing toilet areas—for example, replacing individual urinals by troughs—more area needs to be found to extend the existing provision.

The Upper School Departments (see Figure 5)

73. Following the Sucy-en-Brie exercise logic for retaining specialist accommodation where it is already provided, the basement level should be retained in its entirety. It contains a gymnasium and changing rooms, kitchen and dining room cum theatre (cafetorium), music suite and services plant rooms. Each area was checked for size; the gymnasium was oversized by approximately 80m^2, the dining room was large enough, providing the school works on the basis of four sittings or a continuous self-service cafeteria. (This is not an unusual arrangement in new English schools.) The size of the kitchen seemed to indicate that the present school does not prepare meals but that they arrive pre-packaged for heating on the premises. This arrangement is not normal in English schools although it is operated in some areas; and on this basis the kitchen will be large enough to cope with the number of meals required (80 per cent of pupils assumed—see paragraph 23).

74. The music suite is large enough for the whole school of 1,350 pupils although at least one of the large rooms should, in preference, have a flat floor to give the versatility which the music teachers would, in all likelihood, demand. However, as the tiers exist it is reasonable to accept them. The music suite should preferably be a part of a performing arts department. As the dining room has a stage within it and another enclosed room off it (existing staff room) it would be adequate for the teaching of drama. It is already used as a theatre with good direct access to the outside for escape purposes. The only function of the performing arts department that the existing school does not allow for is the social one. The English model asks for a social base for 50 students but, in this adaptation, an alternative base must be found elsewhere. The only adaptations necessary on this floor would be to meet English fire regulations—new escape doors in the music studio and corridors.

75. On the entrance level (middle level) specialist accommodation is at present provided for the industrial and visual arts. This area already has a suspended floor, a power supply to suit the workshop machinery, direct access to the outside for delivery of bulky materials and protective fire barriers (two-hour fire walls) around it. All the workshops required by the English model could be adequately contained within this area. The position of the existing administrative suite is suitable and the area it occupies can be easily modified to suit the required accommodation. The circulation areas as they exist throughout this and both other floors is excessive by English standards, even taking into consideration the dual use of much of it for personal lockers; every effort would thus have to be made to reduce it to the comparable English amount.

76. Bearing in mind the physical constraints of the block (paragraphs 70 to 72), it was difficult to find a logical split of Upper School accommodation between the two areas on two different levels that would be compatible with the English model. The optimum division seemed to be to accept the link between the technical department, established in the existing industrial and visual arts areas, and to incorporate art, crafts, needlework and home economics into a department on the middle floor around a social area for 160 students. It was decided to include a small social area associated with the technical department to replace that which should have been associated with the performing arts department (refer back to paragraph 74). There was more than adequate floor area to provide these spaces but in order to reduce the amount of circulation, some masonry walls had to be removed. However, it was decided that this was acceptable if it made a significant contribution to the new scheme.

77. In fact, the social areas provided when retaining these masonry walls would have only

Figure 5

Accommodating the English Model

Basis of decisions within the three level block of the Canadian building

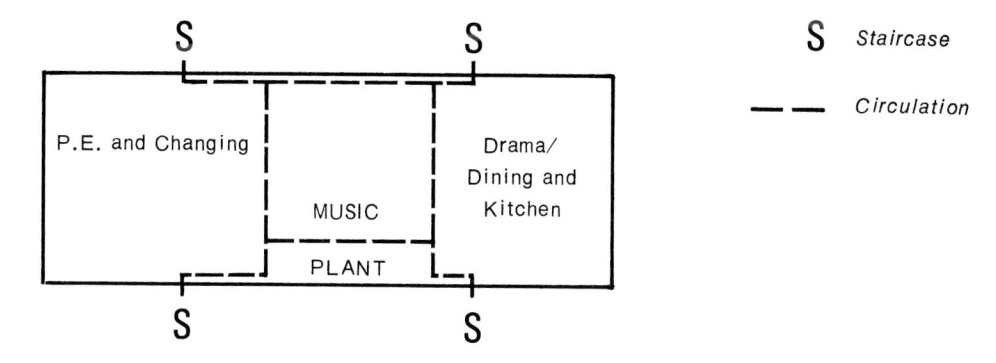

BASEMENT LEVEL
- P.E. and Changing
- MUSIC
- PLANT
- Drama/Dining and Kitchen

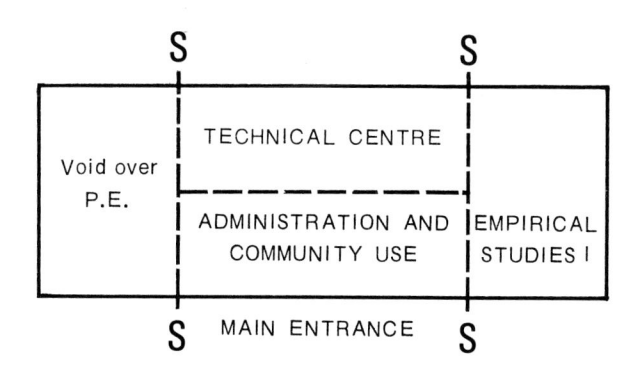

ENTRANCE LEVEL
- Void over P.E.
- TECHNICAL CENTRE
- ADMINISTRATION AND COMMUNITY USE
- EMPIRICAL STUDIES I
- MAIN ENTRANCE

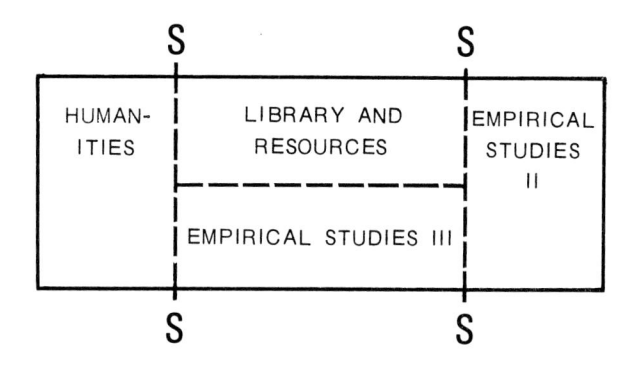

FIRST FLOOR LEVEL
- HUMANITIES
- LIBRARY AND RESOURCES
- EMPIRICAL STUDIES II
- EMPIRICAL STUDIES III

S Staircase
— — Circulation

been suitable for students' personal storage, not for the many other aspects involved in a social area. Unfortunately, the 160-student social area could not be implanted to provide exterior window wall which would give a direct view out of the building and some direct daylight; however, by the use of glazed screens between it and the teaching areas on the perimeter wall it was possible to ensure that it would have some views out of the building. Wherever possible it was decided not totally to enclose teaching areas in the new empirical studies department so that the different teaching areas would flow between each other and the central social area. This was possible to some extent but was limited by the requirements of the fire regulations: all staff-cum-tutorial rooms had to be totally internal due to their small size and the lack of perimeter wall. (As pointed out in the Sucy-en-Brie exercise, this is acceptable as the students are unlikely to spend a considerable time in any of these areas during their working day.)

78. The remainder of the empirical studies areas required by the model were placed in closest proximity to the empirical studies areas on the middle floor—that is, directly above them, on the top floor. It was decided to link the two humanities areas together at the other end of the block on the top floor and to devote the central band between empirical studies and humanities to the library and resources centre: in this way the library and resources centre would serve and link the two. However, in working out the detailed plan, the solution was not so simple: the positions of the stair towers, the necessary circulation between them, and the toilet accommodation off these circulation routes immediately split the floor into a large central area and a smaller area at either end. To suit the diagrammatic breakdown, the area in the centre should have been smaller than the other two areas. The effect on the detail plan was that empirical studies and humanities had each to lose a section to the central area which could operate successfully with the library and resources centre.

79. Physical and living sciences and mathematics were thought to have the strongest links with each other within empirical studies while geography, social studies and economics had more need to be in close relation to the library and resources centre. At the other end of the block, the major difficulty arose in trying to create two separate humanities areas. It seemed more sensible to create a single humanities department and to provide a separate social area in the newly created third empirical studies and library and resources centre in the middle of the block.

80. Other modifications were necessary to the model to solve the planning of both the humanities department and the second empirical studies area. In both, the area available was large enough to provide the number of workplaces necessary but in a much more "open" form than at Sucy-en-Brie in order to make the best use of the deep plan. In this way, the total area for practical work was smaller than at Sucy-en-Brie but by associating practical areas directly to a large shared work area for individual study and seminar groups an acceptable solution was finally arrived at. The effective use of the areas must rely on a different management approach from that implied by the English model.

81. The re-organisation of the administrative suite adjacent to the main entrance created few problems, the general office and reception providing the buffer to the staff accommodation on the left and the community room directly off the foyer to the right. A small interview room was provided off the community room, and an entrance to the medical inspection room so that the community room which could also be used for a careers office, could function as a waiting room or crèche should the need arise.

Summary of Modifications to the English Model (see Figure 6 and Table 8)

82. In the light of the foregoing the following decisions, summarised in note form, were made:

i) No attempt should be made to incorporate the Lower School into the building. It is assumed that a new Lower School for 540 pupils would be built in the vicinity to include the accommodation and facilities described in the original model; it would use the physical education, music, drama, technical crafts and home economics facilities provided for the Upper School.

ii) Accept the dining room and kitchen facilities, the dining room doubling as a drama teaching area.

iii) Accept the music suite.

iv) Accept the gymnasium and changing facilities.

v) Accept the location of the existing Industrial and Visual Arts for the Technical Centre and incorporate a social area.

Figure 6

Revised Model for Arlington

This figure shows the organisation of the pedagogical model revised from that shown in Figure 1 and reflecting the decisions taken and modifications made to the English model.

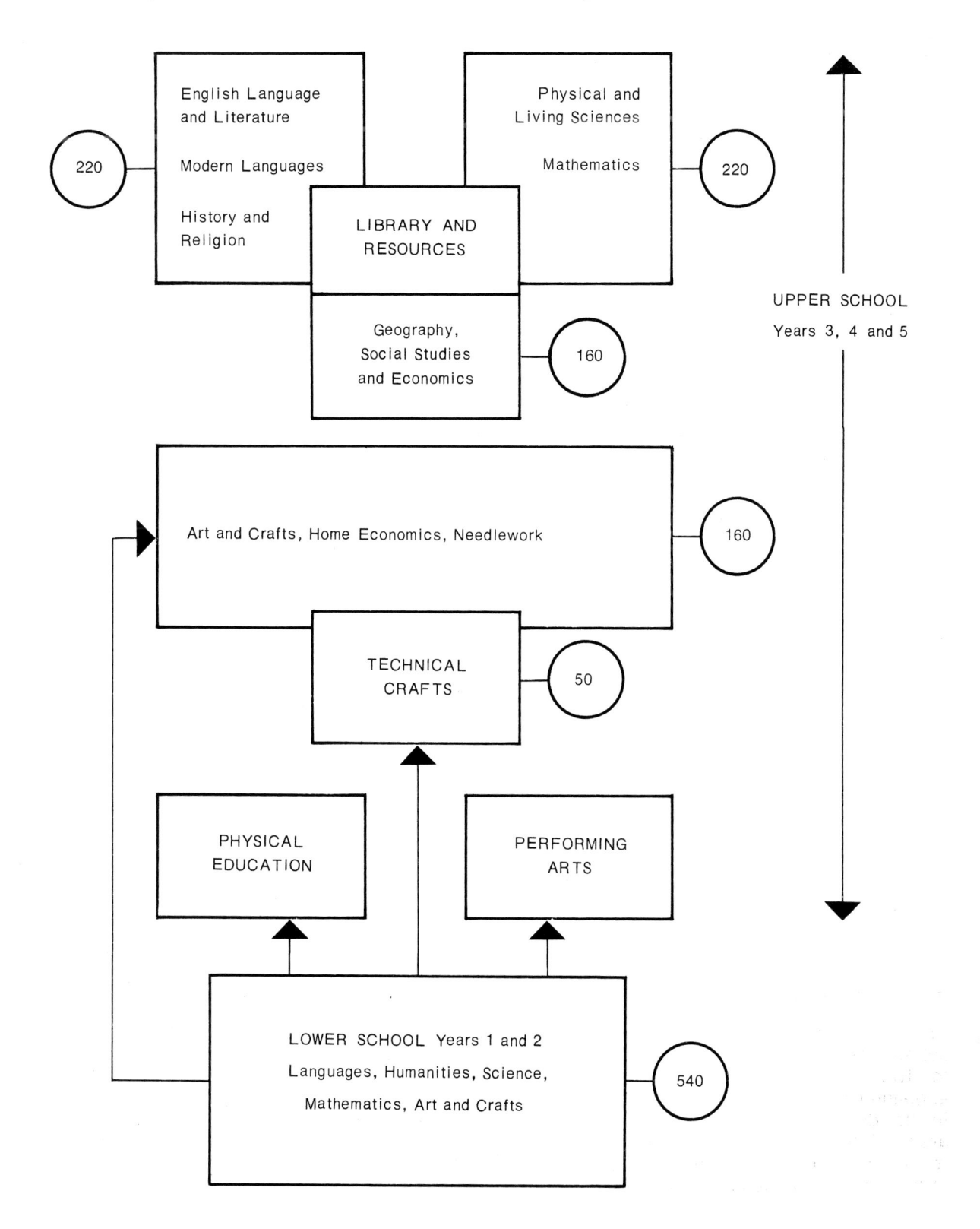

220 — English Language and Literature / Modern Languages / History and Religion	Physical and Living Sciences / Mathematics — 220
LIBRARY AND RESOURCES	
Geography, Social Studies and Economics — 160	

UPPER SCHOOL Years 3, 4 and 5

Art and Crafts, Home Economics, Needlework — 160

TECHNICAL CRAFTS — 50

PHYSICAL EDUCATION

PERFORMING ARTS

LOWER SCHOOL Years 1 and 2
Languages, Humanities, Science, Mathematics, Art and Crafts — 540

vi) Accept the location of the existing administrative suite and make modifications to suit the 1,350 student model.

vii) Empirical Studies Departments:
— art and crafts, needlework, home economics and technical drawing to become a separate department on the middle floor at the south end as empirical studies I;
— sciences and mathematics to become a separate department on the top floor at the south end as empirical studies II;
— geography, economics and social studies to become a separate department adjacent to the library and resources centre in the middle of the top floor as empirical studies III.

viii) Humanities Departments:
— these two departments are combined on the top floor north end as one department.

ix) Social Structure of the School and Community Bases. Departments should incorporate the following social bases:
— Lower School (elsewhere): three bases for 200, 200 and 140 students;
— Upper School

Humanities	220
Empirical Studies I	160
Empirical Studies II	220
Empirical Studies III	160
Technical Centre	50

Table 8
Arlington. Revised Distribution of Workplaces and Social Places.

In the following table, the distribution of workplaces and social places is amended from that shown in Table 3 to reflect the decisions taken and modifications made to the English model.

	Humanities	Empirical Studies I	Empirical Studies II	Empirical Studies III	Performing Arts	Technical Centre	Physical Education	Lower School
English	90				25			70
Modern Languages	70							40
History	45							30
Religion and Philosophy	45							30
Geography, etc.				68				44
Mathematics			115					70
Science			133					60
Art and Crafts		90						36
Needlework		44						
Home Economics		66						
Music					75			
Drama					42			
Wood and Metalwork						88		
Technical Drawing		22						
Physical Education							68 indoor 68 outdoor	
Library, Resources and Study	30	25	30	25		10		30
Social Places	220	160	220	160		50		200 200 140

The Solution (Plans 18 to 20 inclusive)

83. The English model of a comprehensive school used in this exercise has been applied to two quite different building forms. As explained elsewhere, there is nothing absolute in its demands other than a total teaching area. Within this total, considerable variation is possible to suit different forms of school organisation and teaching methods. In the Sucy-en-Brie adaptation, a successful design solution has been achieved by only slight variation of the model. In the case of the Arlington school however, the attempt to achieve a comparable proportion and variety of closed teaching spaces, together with the environmental guidelines laid down for school building in England, has resulted in a less profitable use of the floor space than would otherwise be the case.

84. A more advantageous solution might have been reached through a more open interpretation of the English model and a greater use of mobile furniture and storage units to articulate the space. However, by imposing English fire regulations to this adaptation, it is doubtful whether a more open solution could have been found without constructing more fire escapes from the building.

85. For purposes of comparison, both these studies have been tied to the same educational model. In those countries where considerable variation of accommodation is permitted and where architects can freely interpret the wishes of their clients, it is conceivable that a quite different approach to adaptation might be made. A design team faced with adapting a particular building to new educational purposes would evolve a model best suited to that building. This assumes a design team with educators appointed to safeguard educational interests and objectives. Had this been done in the Arlington study, a more advantageous solution might have resulted. Thus, while an existing building is a constraint upon designers, the degree of such constraint will depend upon their freedom to evolve an educational model which exploits its space and facilities to the greatest advantage.

72

Plan 18 : **ARLINGTON ENGLISH MODE**

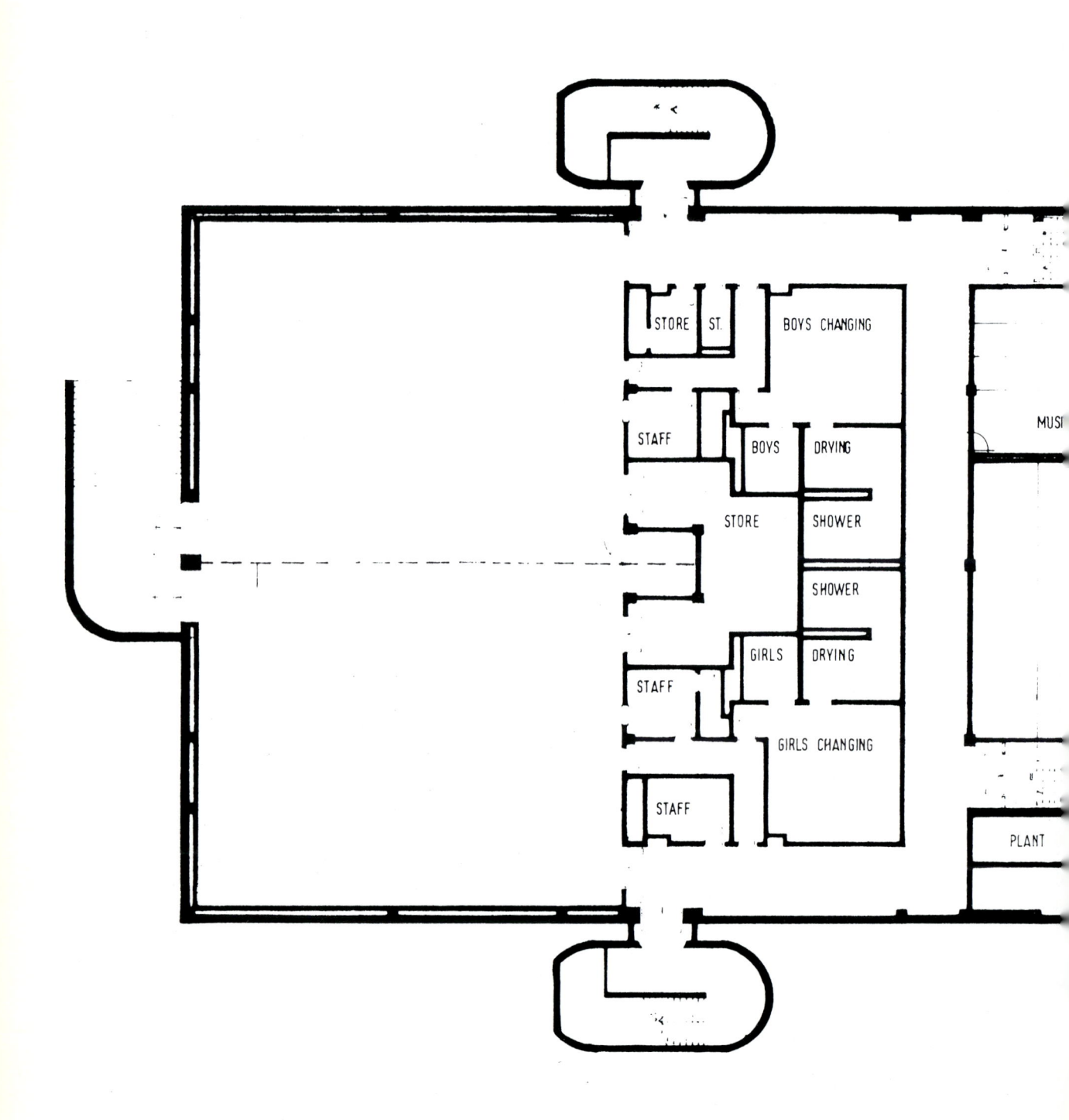

BASEMENT LEVEL

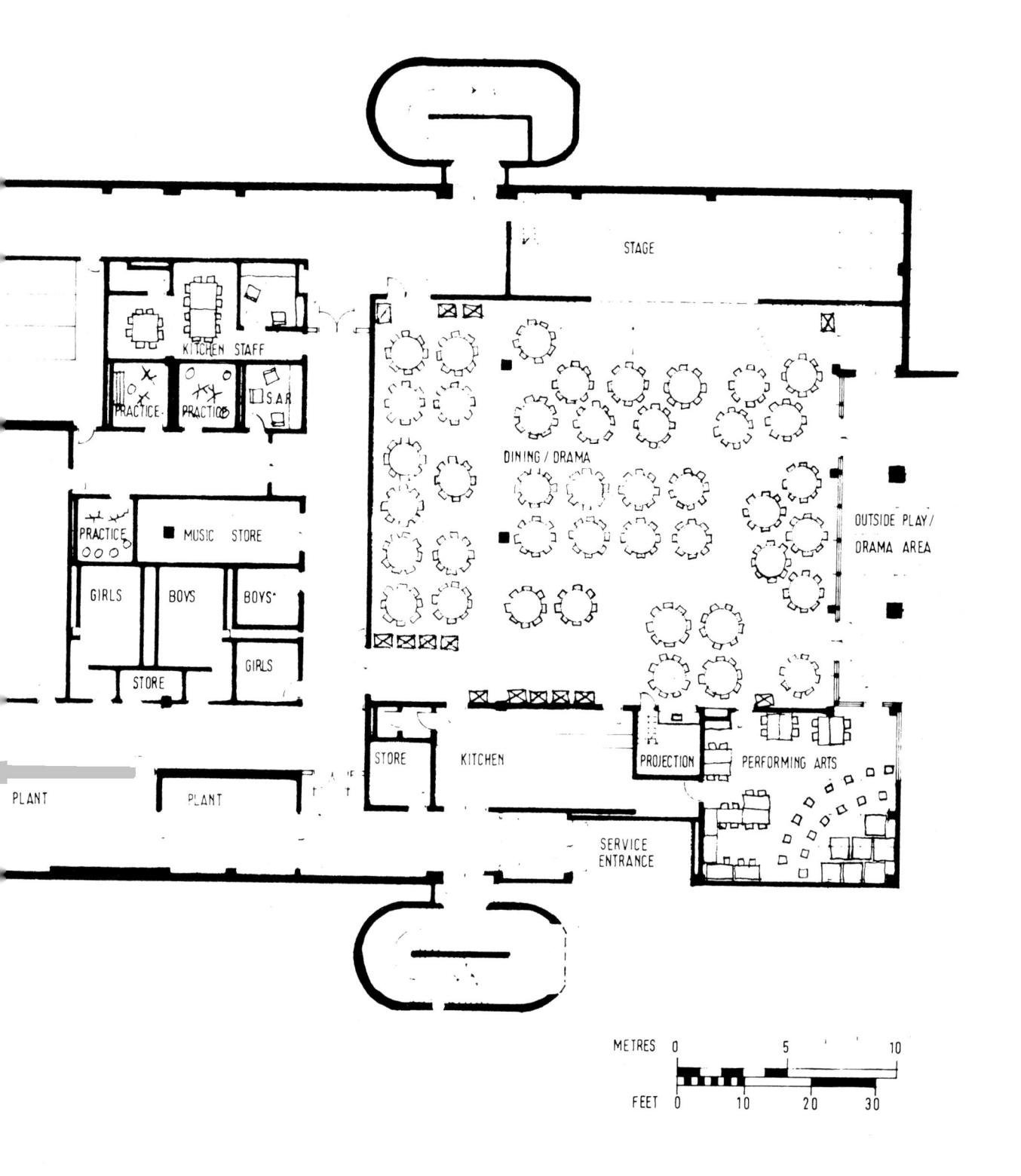

Plan 19 : **ARLINGTON ENGLISH MODE**

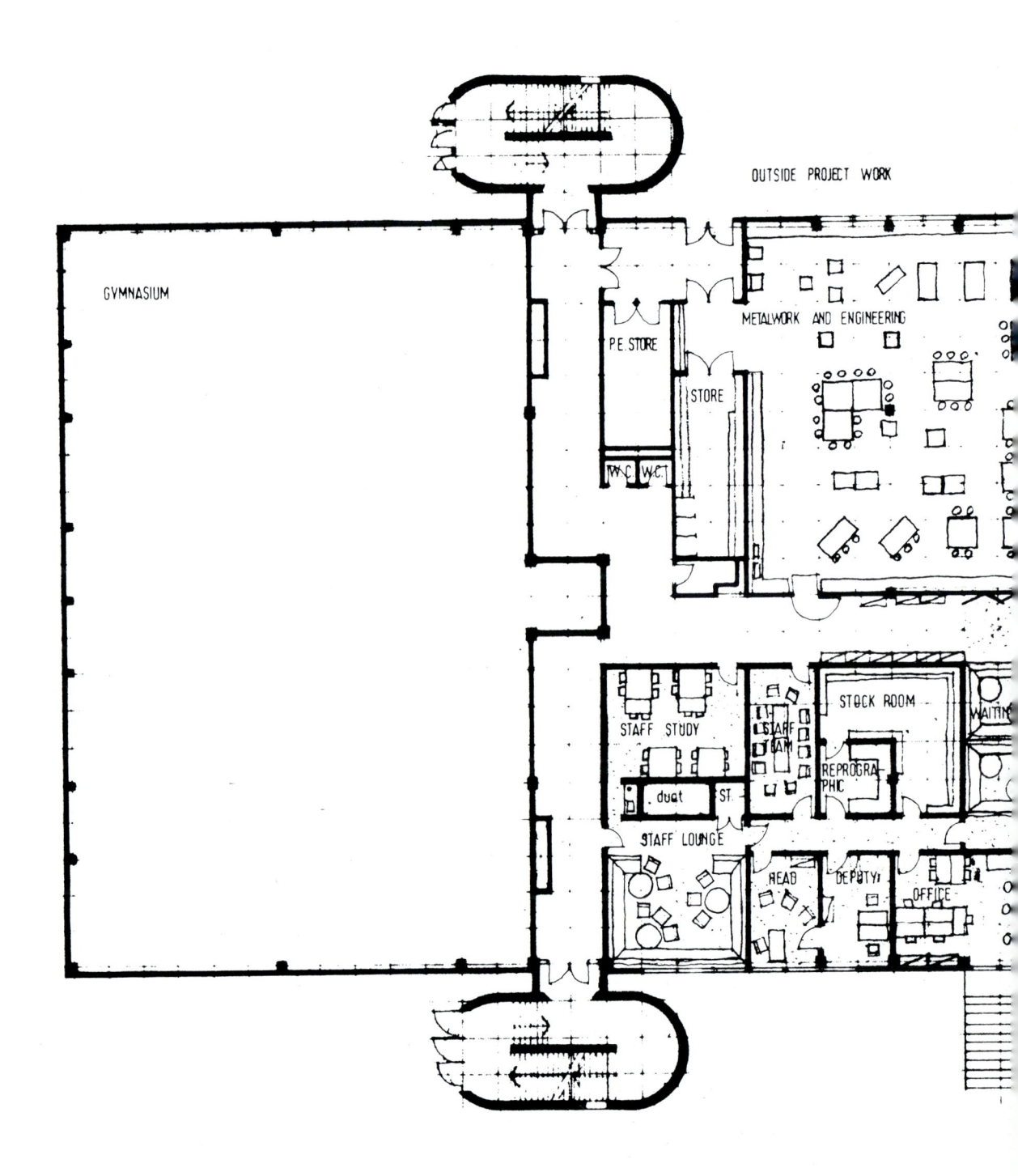

ENTRANCE LEVEL

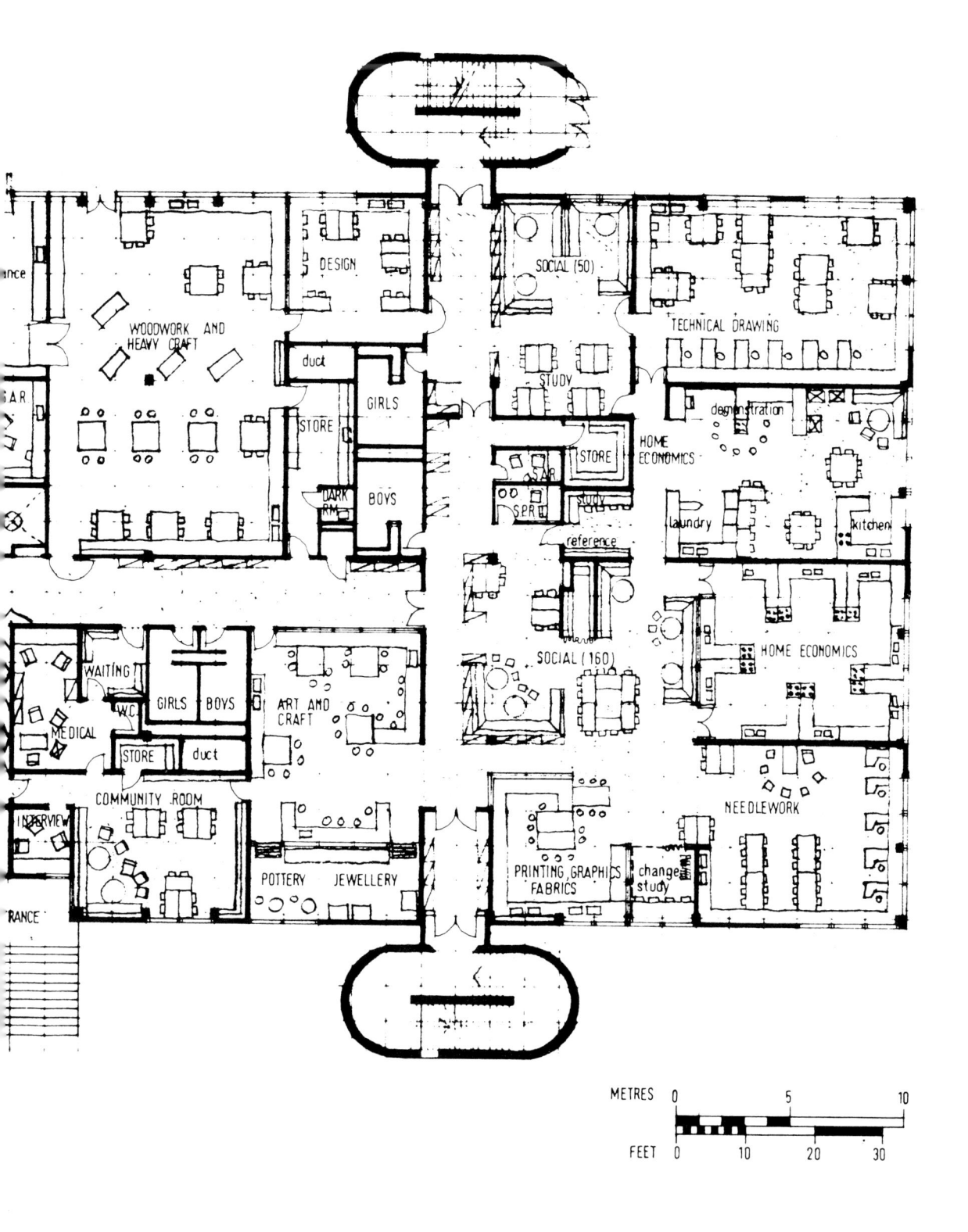

Plan 20 : **ARLINGTON ENGLISH MODEL**

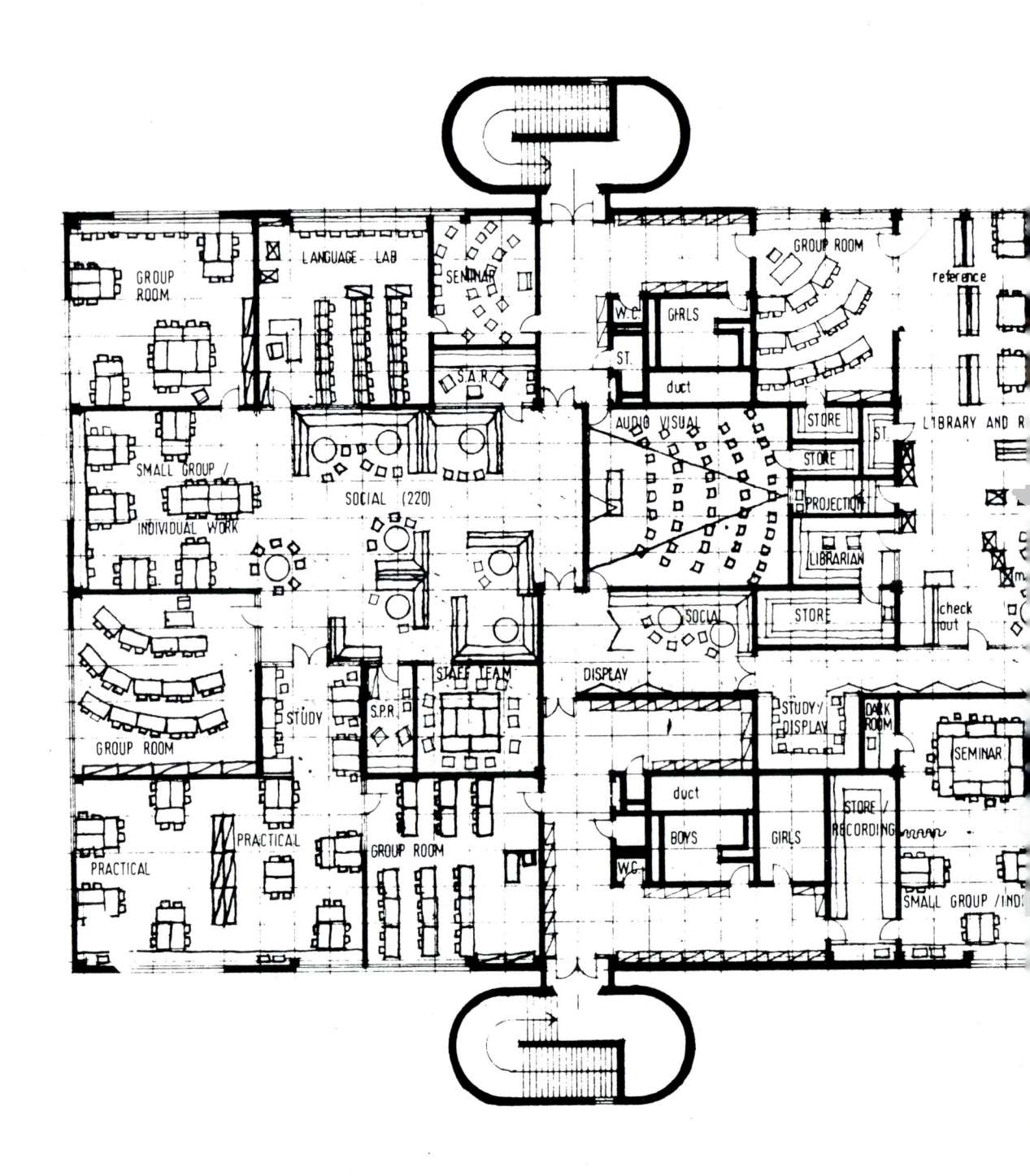

FIRST FLOOR LEVEL

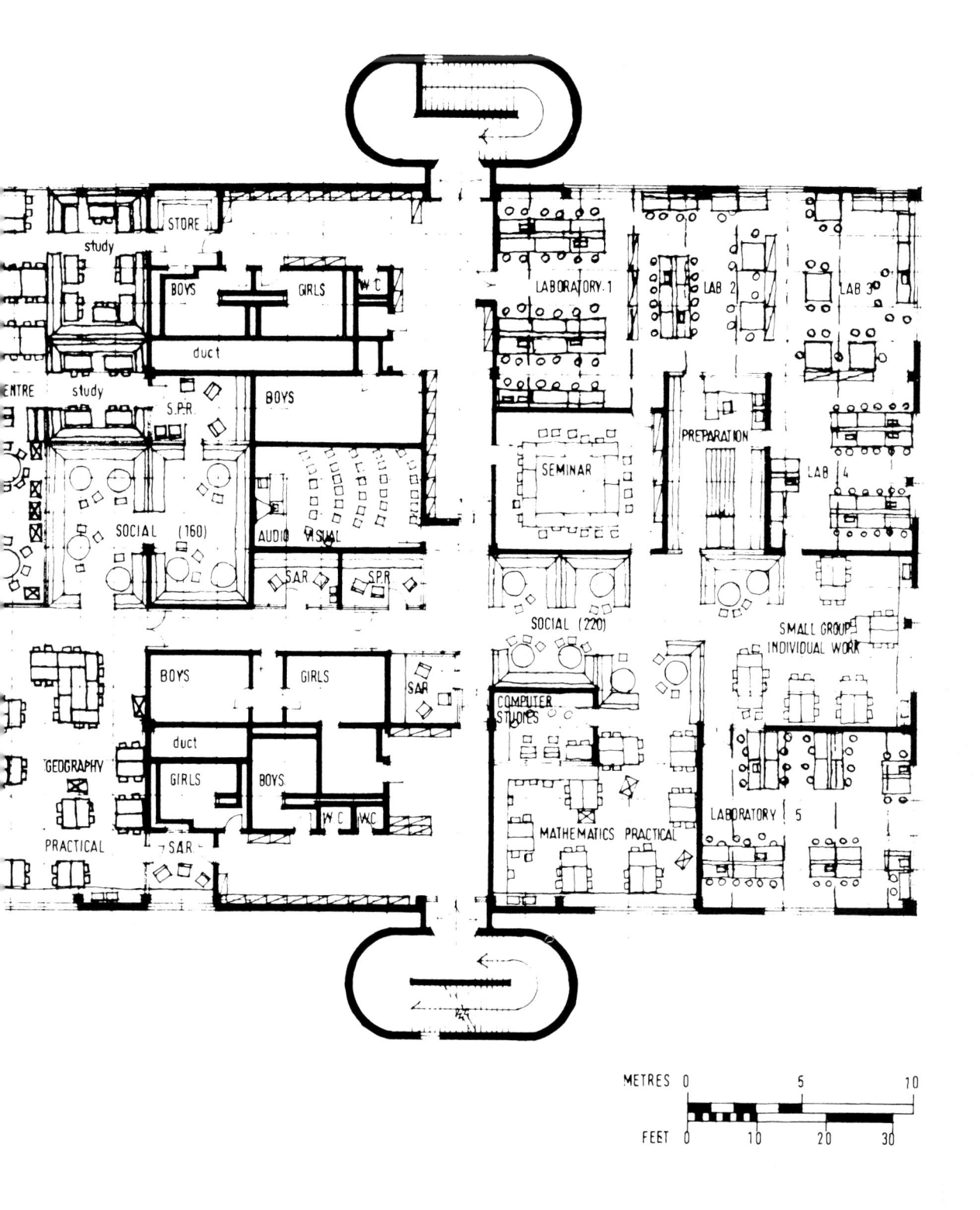

Degrees of Adaptability

86. The following summarises the qualities of the Arlington school in meeting the changes which the English model school demanded.

Adaptable features

i) The large floor area on each level.
ii) The ability to add, replace or remove internal partitions indepently of the structure of the building.
iii) The ceiling servicing enables the repositioning of the partitions almost anywhere—no restrictions are imposed on the re-organisation due to the fixed position of services.
iv) The dispersed toilet accommodation.
v) Uninterrupted floor areas due to the large structural spans allowed freedom of positioning large teaching areas—lecture rooms, audio-visual rooms.

Unadaptable features

i) Circulation routes across the block dictated by the positions of the stair towers and toilet blocks cut the block into three separate areas.
ii) The length of the block demands a linear circulation pattern along its length.
iii) The width of the block means that some teaching areas cannot comply with the DES Guidelines for daylighting and that in any re-organisation of the building the perimeter wall is at a premium.
iv) The size of the block is such that to comply with English fire regulations a degree of compartmentation is necessary especially on the top floor. This inhibits the optimum use of the deep plan internal space.
v) The fixed two-hour fire walls on either side of existing cross circulation routes were too restrictive to the re-organisation of the school and to suit the English model some had to be removed.

Table 9
Area Analysis of Arlington as Existing.

	Basement Level	Entrance Level	First Floor Level	Total	Percentage
Teaching	283.35	994.50	1,838.96	3,116.81	42.39
Ancillary	339.09	144.00	153.29	636.38	8.66
Administration	86.40	270.80	144.14	501.34	6.82
Circulation	624.94	621.69	573.38	1,820.01	24.76
Dining	473.79			473.79	6.44
Kitchen	102.19			102.19	1.39
Boilers, plant	97.55			97.55	1.33
Gymnasium	603.85			603.85	8.21
Total	2,611.16	2,030.99	2,709.77	7,351.92	100.00

Table 10
Area Analysis of Arlington English Model.

	Basement Level	Entrance Level	First Floor Level	Total	Percentage
Teaching	355.81	1,160.79	1,905.52	3,422.12	46.28
Ancillary	339.09	172.79	304.25	816.13	11.04
Administration	13.94	235.04	1.40	250.38	3.38
Circulation	624.94	505.56	498.60	1,629.10	22.03
Dining	473.79			473.79	6.41
Kitchen	102.19			102.19	1.38
Boilers, Plant	97.55			97.55	1.32
Gymnasium	603.85			603.85	8.16
Total	2,611.16	2,074.18	2,709.77	7,395.11	100.00

Part three
IMPLICATIONS OF PROVIDING FOR CHANGE

87. The closely inter-related nature of the problems considered is reflected in the content of this Part Three. Certain factors thus crop up under more than one heading, although every attempt has been made to avoid needless repetition. The aim of the somewhat artificial breakdown is to present the work and its findings in as clear and immediate a way as possible while at the same time bringing out this close inter-relationship.

INSTITUTIONAL AND MANAGERIAL ARRANGEMENTS

88. To treat the problems of providing for future change as a technological issue alone is to obscure other equally important factors. The most important of these factors stem from the ability inherent in organisations—in the present context school communities, though others have the same ability—to themselves adapt to non "tailor-made" buildings.

89. In the report on the Multi-Option School, Jean Ader notes that, in the planning and design of school buildings, educational needs are not such that they can be simply translated into activities and then into closely matching facilities: there can be no one-for-one correspondence between the types of activities desired and the types of facilities provided for them. He observes that, in practice, "...desirable activities are never defined from scratch but usually from a critical examination of educational practice in which elements of innovation can be discerned. Furthermore, the possible is defined by the tension between what is desired and the identified constraints".[1] He goes on to point out that the "...possible must not be conceived solely as an impoverishment of the desirable; experience in fact shows that facilities are capable of accommodating activities which had not been foreseen..."[2] and that the "...contraints do not all concern the building or its envisaged equipment, but... include, for example, the availability and qualifications of the teachers and their ability to adapt".[3]

90. That individuals and organisations are themselves adaptable should be stressed, so that in working out schemes for adaptation, something may safely be left and, indeed, should be left to their resourcefulness and ingenuity. Although design has a great deal to offer, management has a most important contribution to make in exploiting the opportunities for change within a building through its organisation and use of the facilities available.

91. Two examples can be cited.

---

1. Jean Ader, *Building Implications of the Multi-Option School,* OECD, Paris, 1975, paragraph 83.
2. Ader, *op. cit.*
3. Ader, *op. cit.*

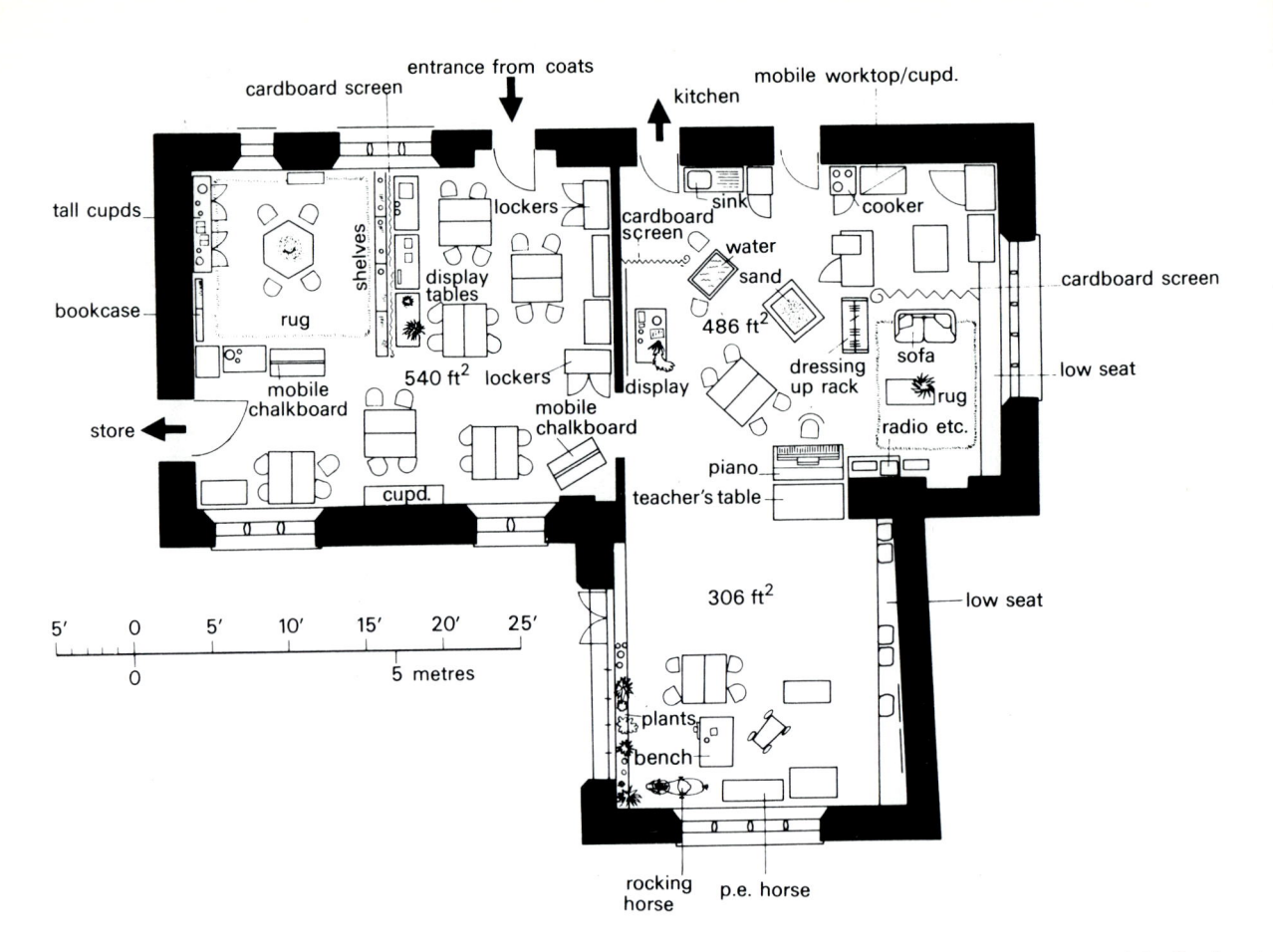

Figure 7: **An old primary school (erected in 1871) adapted to new educational demands at modest cost to the local authority. Some improvements to the building and a lot of ingenuity on the part of the teachers have given the school a more informal and homelike character.**

i) Where a secondary school has been organised in a complex of detached buildings, and this frequently happens in the creation of large multi-option schools, directors and teaching staff so organise the teaching programmes that pupils spend several periods, or even whole days, within a particular building block. To further this, improvisations are often made to broaden the range of educational facility within the blocks. By so doing, school management is demonstrating that schools can be effectively conducted in detached buildings and that the expansion of teaching accommodation and facilities into institutional buildings other than schools is feasible. Thus, solutions rest with school management as well as with designers.

ii) Where the initial design has failed to provide study areas, seminar and discussion spaces or practical workplaces for incidental use, for developing forms of education in which pupils play an active, participating role, management often improvises them. This can be seen in many older buildings where circulation space and other non-teaching areas have been adapted to such purposes by the director and teachers of the school.[1] In the United Kingdom, some very successful Sixth Form Centres (for students of 16 to 18 years of age) have been created in large dwelling houses with little building adaptation.

1. Needless to say, such improvisation does not obviate the need in each case to take account of or comply with fire or safety regulations specific to each country.

Figure 8: **Another example of change initiated by teachers and requiring but modest financial support from the local authority: the previous circulation and cloakroom area between classrooms has been converted to an open study area through some minor alterations.**

92. Linked with the above is the need for flexibility of mind in attempting to introduce a new educational model into an existing building. Suppose, for example, that such a model suggests at first sight the need for a single library/resource centre serving the whole school. In the Arlington example this proved quite feasible. But with Sucy-en-Brie, the existing form of the building meant that the value of such an arrangement would be offset by consequential extraneous movement which could easily discourage the habit of using the resources. To adapt the building to overcome this disadvantage would not be economically feasible, whereas reconsideration of the educational premise showed that the educational objectives would be met, not only equally but possibly even better by dispersing library/resource facilities so as to form resource *foci* for each department of the school. Hence a fixed educational model, to be applied regardless of the physical circumstances, is not likely to maximise the potential of an existing building or to get the best from such adaptation as might be practical. Flexibility of mind on the part of educational management is essential in seeking the most appropriate solution.

93. Here, however, it will be apparent that management, in seeking to accommodate new pedagogical models into existing buildings, needs to work closely with designers who know what is or is not physically practical. In this respect the adaptation of existing facilities imposes tasks which resemble those of providing new buildings. In both cases it is necessary first, that school building designers tap the direct experience of the day-to-day decision-making that goes into the use of school building on the part of directors and teachers and second, that school building users are made aware of the possibilities offered by the physical facilities at their disposal. The crucial part that close designer/user collaboration can play is self-evident.

94. This seeing the desirable in the light of the feasible, this need for designer/user collaboration jointly to explore physically possible solutions, this flexibility of mind required on the part of educational management applies then to the provision and use of physical facilities whether new buildings, adapted ones or existing. At any one time, new school buildings can only be a proportion—usually a small one—of all school buildings or, indeed, of all buildings. As such, they need to be considered as additions to an existing stock and need looking at not in isolation but in relation to other built facilities existing or proposed in their locality. The flexibility which results from the location and co-ordination (or integration) of school facilities with housing, other public buildings (libraries, welfare centres, social clubs), workshops and commercial buildings can be of great importance in any policy aimed at facing the problems of future change.

95. All the foregoing managerial factors essentially concern the malleability of organisations and their requirements and their capacity for compromise. It is difficult to measure what, if anything, is lost by such compromises. This study can hardly pursue the question further but must concentrate mainly on what can be done now to avoid constructing buildings which will not prove amenable to change. Nevertheless these wider considerations need a mention here if only to underline the importance of seeing physical needs in a broader perspective.

SPACE SUB-DIVISION AND LAYOUT

96. Work on the Maiden Erlegh case example clearly demonstrates that certain spatial layouts can, without physical alteration, successfully serve many quite different purposes (although all the purposes are admittedly educational in one way or another). Likewise, the possibilities for adaptation studied in both the Sucy-en-Brie and the Arlington examples are aimed at satisfying the flexibility in use demanded by the new educational model being housed. It is difficult, however, to be precise or scientifically certain about what exactly makes for this flexibility (as defined in paragraph 5) or within what limits of future change the degree of flexibility would remain effective. Nevertheless some pointers can be discerned.

97. The process of learning involves pupils and teachers in a pattern of different activities; traditionally these are reading, writing, talking and listening but nowadays they include painting, making pottery, modelling, scientific experiments, cooking, looking after animals and so on in an almost endless list—see, for example, Table 4 on page 00 for an idea of the enormous range of such activities. Now, a great many of these educational activities can be performed while sitting at a table—for example, reading, writing, listening through headphones to a tape-recorder, looking at a miniaturised slide-projector—without disturbance to others. Furthermore, recent developments in mobile furniture have made it possible to increase the range of activities which such a workplace can serve, by supplementing it as need be with, for example, a painting easel or even by a mobile sink, or by providing additional tables or pushing the tables from several workplaces together. Because they serve so many activities such workplaces can be called basic.

98. Now the value of a **basic workplace** is enhanced first if not too far away from it is a resource area providing easy access to more books, or slides, or recording tapes than any single basic workplace can contain. Its value is further increased by equal proximity to, for example, a blackboard on which large diagrams can be quickly drawn and just as quickly altered, or to a display area where, say, the behaviour of life in an aquarium can be studied. For many purposes the random and occasional movement between the basic workplace and these supplementary facilities does not disturb others who are pursuing similar activities; and for such purposes a large number of basic workplaces can be situated in an undivided general space. But for other purposes, even when the activities are similar, some degree of enclosure may be needed—for example to give privacy for remedial teaching, or for predominantly expository teaching. Basic workplaces then need to be contained within a space which provides such privacy. Thus a distinction can be made between **committed spaces** of this kind and **general spaces**, the size of which are limited and governed not by the number of occupants but by ease of access from basic workplaces to associated facilities and from the general space to the committed spaces associated with its use.

99. **Specialised workplaces** can be distinguished by the fact that they provide some facility which lies beyond the scope of a basic workplace, however it may be supplemented. Advanced science may require experimental facilities such as fume cupboards or expensive equipment needing special protection or safeguards in use. Technical activities like metalwork or joinery need similarly specialised equipment. Almost invariably where workplaces have to be specialised in such ways

Figure 9: **A number of basic workplaces situated in an undivided general space, providing easy access to resources and allowing occasional movement by pupils with no or little disturbance.**

Figure 10: **An example of basic workplaces in a committed space providing the privacy needed for certain types of activities.**

Figure 11: **Specialised workplaces: learning to type, and the audio-visual method used in this particular case, not only demand specialised equipment but also an environment which is specialised (here: the acoustic treatment).**

their use demands an environment which is specialised also (for example, acoustic treatment, special floor finishes, dust extraction) and which, as a consequence, again requires the provision of committed space.

100. Physical education of the kind which requires wall-ladders, climbing ropes or other fixed apparatus is another example; but even without such apparatus, the boisterous and possibly noisy activity involved will necessitate space being specially committed to it. To this, however, there is an important exception: provided a general space is equipped with sufficiently mobile furniture that a sufficient floor area can be cleared, and provided no other activity occurs there at the same time, then it too can be used for physical education, as it may be used for musical or dramatic activity.

101. The more basic places can be supplemented by other facilities in a general space the greater the number of activities which can occur there. The greater the proportion of general to committed space the greater the opportunity for varying activity patterns. But it must be remembered that, in practice general space can not contain all activities. Furthermore, the wider the range of specialised workplaces available the wider the range of opportunity for diversifying the activities which can be pursued. Thus a building which initially contains only a narrow range of specialised workplaces is more likely to require modification to suit future change than one where the range is so wide that almost every imaginable activity can be undertaken. But for many of these specialised workplaces committed spaces will be needed. Thus while flexibility will increase with the proportion of

general to committed space the proportion can not be maximised but only optimised, due regard being paid to the educational needs.

102. There is however a further aspect of flexibility to be considered, namely the allowance for some "slack" in the number of workplaces provided for a given number of pupils. If all pupils in a school are engaged all the time on one activity alone then the number of identical workplaces needed will equal the number of pupils. Even in such a simple theoretical situation, however, some flexibility would still be required unless overcrowding or under-use were to accompany the variations in school enrolment which are inevitable. The same requirement arises when, as in reality, pupils engage in more than one activity. The more the number of workplaces exceeds the normal number of pupils, the greater the flexibility.

103. In theory, if all pupils spend 20 per cent of their time on activity A, 40 per cent on B and 40 per cent on C, then 20 per cent of all workplaces should be for activity A, 40 per cent for B and 40 per cent for C. In more general terms, the proportion of all workplaces devoted to a specific activity should be the same as the proportion of all pupil-hours devoted to the activity. In practice, exigencies of time-tabling themselves dependent on staff availability and on the way learning activities are to be organised, mean that in a given period a higher percentage of pupils may be engaged in an activity. Thus, again, the flexibility will be proportional to the excess of the real number of workplaces for an activity over the theoretical percentage of pupils engaged on it.

104. The pointers towards flexibility can now be summarised. In essence flexibility will be maximised according to the extent to which it proves feasible:

a) to provide an excess of workplaces over the number of occupants;
b) to widen the range of activities which general space can accommodate, by means of supplementary facilities, especially mobile furniture and equipment to increase the scope of basic workplaces;
c) to widen the range of specialised workplaces in order to widen the range of opportunity;
d) to optimise the proportion of general to committed space.

None of these measures must be seen as a justification for increased costs. They can be achieved by the considered distribution of financial resources within existing expenditure limits (see paragraphs 157 to 159 inclusive).

105. The greater the flexibility the less the need for adaptation. But clearly educational change may be of an order of magnitude which exceeds the limits when flexibility can provide for it. When this order of magnitude is reached it will be because the educational change introduces new activities which require further specialised workplaces to be added to the range, or require a change in the proportion of specialised to basic or between one kind of specialised and another. And this in turn may require changes in what spaces have to be committed.

106. Such conversion, of course brings into play the capacity of the building for physical alteration—in short, its adaptability. A striking fact to emerge from the study of developments directed towards increased adaptability is that adaptability is almost invariably seen first in terms of relocatable partitions. Doubtless this stems from the belief that the demand for physical alteration arises from a need to alter the pattern of internal spaces which partitions demarcate and separate and that the occupants of school buildings frequently want to change the size and shape of rooms. However, the foregoing analysis will have shown that the importance of partitions is chiefly in enclosing committed space. The case studies have shown that where the balance between committed and general is optimal the need to remove or add partitions is small. Because this principle has not been understood the importance attached to relocatable partitions as the key to adaptability has been based on a serious misconception or over-simplification of real educational need.

107. Granted, the traditional accommodation for most indoor activities is some kind of room—classroom, laboratory, office, gymnasium, lavatory, workshop—and the boundary to both accommodation and activity is formed by walls. But consideration not only of changes in activity which may occur but also of changes in behaviour which are already occuring in schools raise questions as to why this should continue to be the case. The acoustic conditions needed, for example, in a school designed for flexibility will demand an awareness that, in many cases, much less time is spent nowadays listening to the teacher "giving a lesson", or in question and answer sessions—teaching modes which demand that only one person should speak at a time while the rest remain quiet if not attentive. The

acoustic behaviour which should determine the acoustic environment is quite different with the learning modes now common where pupils are engaged on individual or group activity with the teacher moving from one individual or group to another. In this case, the acoustic behaviour is what may be described as "conversational"; a background of conversation is quite acceptable when in the other example it would be just the reverse.

108. Partition walls then may or may not constitute an essential facility for the activity concerned—freedom from distraction, visual or aural, security against theft or damage to expensive equipment, essential display or writing surfaces, support for equipment or apparatus, etc. On the other hand, they clearly limit the size of pupil group and militate against any association or interplay of activities which may be desirable.

109. Certainly, in the design exercises carried out under this study there are many instances where partitions in the existing buildings are removed to make larger spaces or new ones inserted for sub-division. But the exercises also show that the size and shape of spaces is only one inhibition, and often a minor one, when it is sought to change educational methods or introduce new activities. In practice, the demand is usually more challenging: for extra services, especially water supply and drainage serving additional sinks for purposes of painting or clay-modelling or for "scientific experiments"; or for electricity supply to illustrate aspects of science again or to facilitate the use of audio-visual aids.

110. The same desire to extend the range of educational activity creates a demand for different kinds of floor finish which, for example, will not inhibit "dirty" or "messy" activities

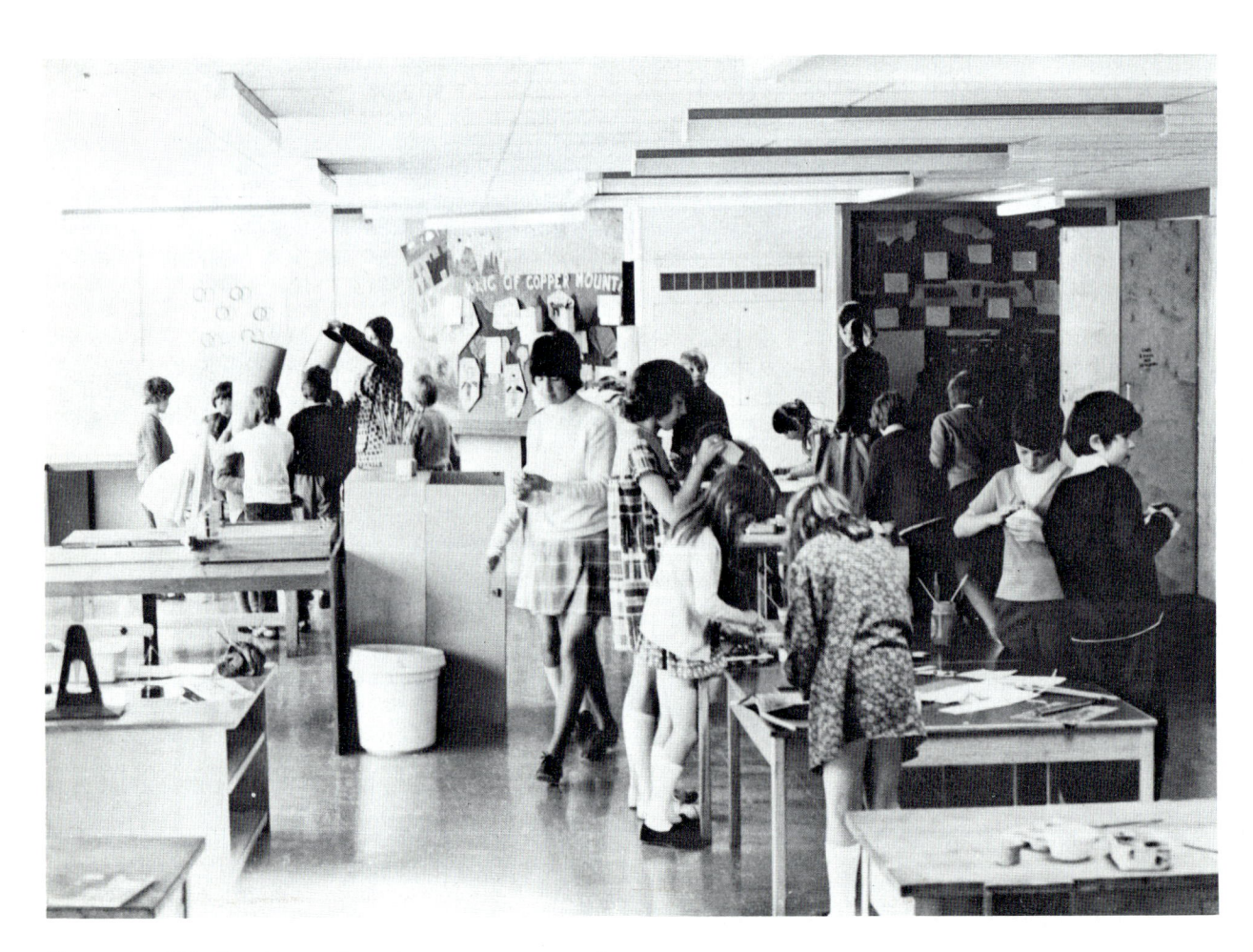

Figure 12: **"Dirty" or "messy" activities require special floor finishes which do not inhibit such activities.**

Figure 13: **Other activities need a floor finish which can help create a domestic-type ambiance facilitating relationships as in this case between the child and his teacher.**

or, conversely, which will encourage children to sit on the floor as the more fortunate among them might sit on a fireside rug to listen to a story told at home. The demand may equally be for new light sources or for darkening a naturally lit room in order to see slide or film projections or create special lighting effects for a drama group; or for extra sound-absorption to reduce the noise level resulting from more active learning processes. These are the demands which adaptability, if it is to be useful, must turn to satisfying and the report returns to them later under the heading "Environment and Services".

111. That concentration on the relocatability of partitions is largely a misconception is thus evident. But it is also a dangerous misconception and one which is strangely paradoxical. The first danger is that it can be wasteful of limited resources, diverting them from more profitable use. This danger is further increased by the fact that when partitions are relocatable many other expensive consequences follow affecting, for example, the structure of the building and its internal environment—consequences which are gone into in more detail under the appropriate headings. The second danger follows from the first and gives rise to the paradox: the search for adaptability in room shape and size and the resolution of the problems arising from its consequences for the structure and environment can lead to a uniformity in every characteristic of the school environment—adaptability where it is least required and no adaptability in the directions where education demands it.

PLAN FORM AND BUILDING ENVELOPE

112. Where the major activity in school is one where pupils, arranged in uniform classes, sit at desks, listen to expositions by a teacher and write verbal or numerical exercises while seated at the same desks, the physical accommodation needed is simple and well understood and buildings perfectly suited to it are essentially strings of uniform classrooms connected by a corridor—like compartments in a railway carriage. Just as the length of the carriage is in essence a multiple of the compartment so are the overall dimensions of the building a multiple of the classroom.

113. But where educational activity is increasingly diverse—which is the case in most countries—accommodation becomes much more diverse and the plan form less predictable or regular. Expressions of this development are to be seen in many of the post-war schools built in England with their irregular plan forms with frequently indented perimeters. To dissect all the underlying motivations would be to digress from the subject; it is enough to single out two specific aims: first, to provide a rich variety of environment and secondly, to so shape the building that it differentiates and shelters outdoor teaching space—seen in the English climate as a useful extension and complement to indoor space.

114. Because such indented perimeter forms, with their high ratio of external wall to floor area, are inherently costly, other ways of providing environmental variety and sheltered outdoor space are also to be seen. Allied to these ways is the adoption of the deep plan with varying degrees of mechanical ventilation

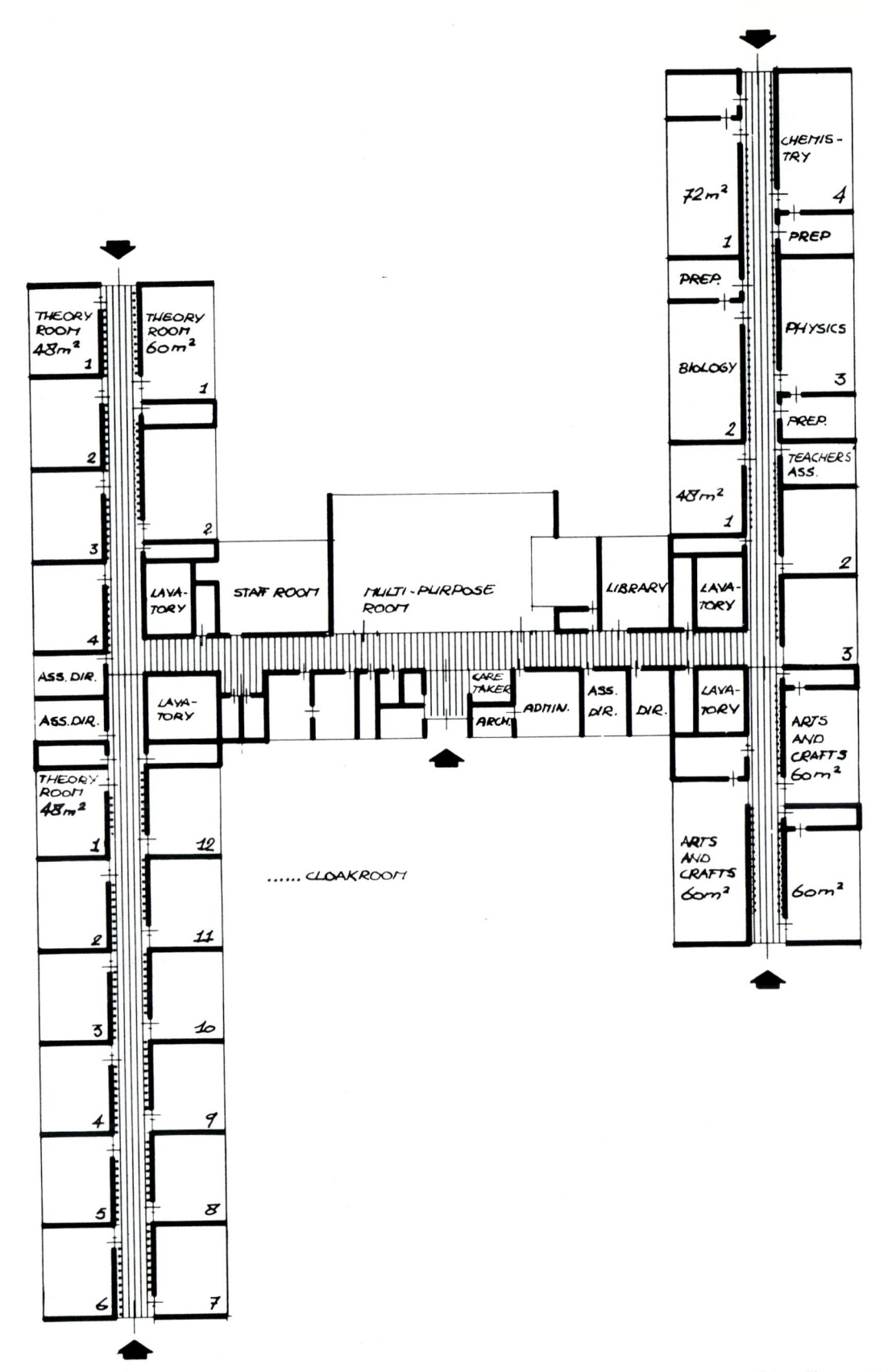

Figure 14: An example of a traditional type of design: uniform classrooms connected by a corridor, like compartments in a railway carriage; such buildings are perfectly suited when the major activity in school consists in listening to expositions by a teacher or in writing verbal or numerical exercises while seated at the same desk...

115. Now, all these typical plan forms, each meeting the demands of a different approach to education, have implications for adaptability and flexibility. The accommodation of any one of the approaches to education represented within the plan forms of the others is unlikely to be achieved with total success. But, accepting that educational demands on school building are governed as much by the feasible as by the desirable, does one plan form favour such change more than another—either without physical alteration, that is by its flexibility, or with physical alteration, that is using the and reliance on artificial lighting to supplement daylight. Many recent English schools, for example, tend to be a series of blocks planned as one or more regular rectangles—the Maiden Erlegh Lower School block illustrated in Part Two of this report is one such block. In other countries, notably Canada, Sweden and the United States, such "regular rectangle" plan forms are likewise common—although they tend to be deeper in plan than their English counterparts and place more reliance on artificial lighting and ventilation (see, for example, Arlington).

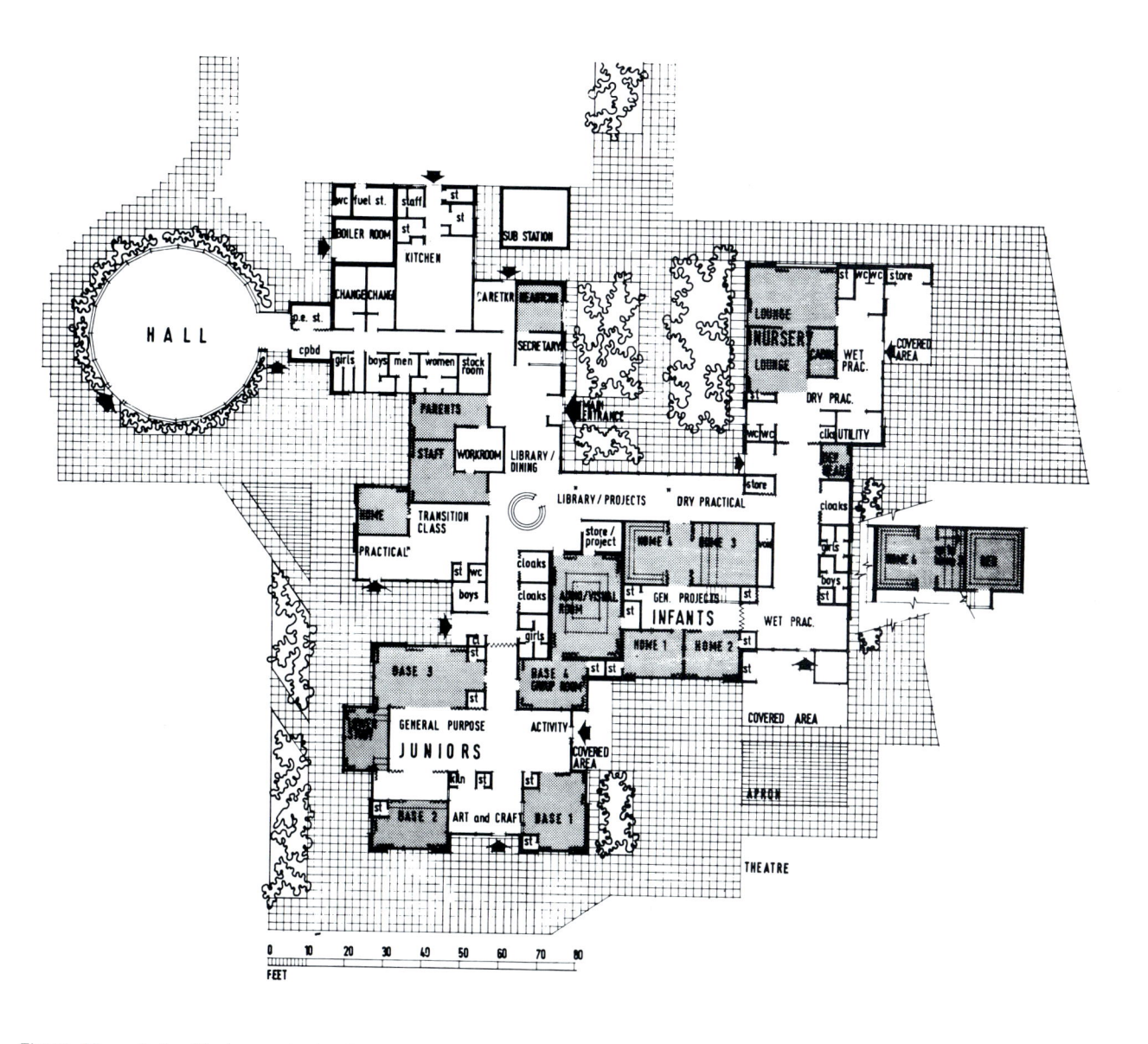

Figure 15: ...but with increasingly diverse educational activities accommodation needs to be much more diverse and hence requires less predictable or regular plan forms as in this example with its frequently indented perimeter.

qualities of adaptability it offers? And, assuming that it does, what are the features that enable this?

116. Work on the design exercises, in which changes of this sort were actually carried out, reveals some of these features. First of all, it must be recognised that the plan form of any building is not something which is arbitrarily selected at the whim of the designer: this much is obvious. A major determinant in all cases is the internal spatial layout, discussed previously, and the consideration of educational activity which gives rise to it.

117. The study of any particular educational topic, irrespective of whether the topic is subject-oriented or interdisciplinary, may demand that several activities alternate with each other in quick succession—theory alternating with practice, for example, or one kind of practical work with another. If work is not to be disrupted, the different types of accommodation needed for alternating activities must be close to one another. At the same time, some of the activities (and thus the accommodation needed for them) may be associated with only one educational topic, while other activities may be associated with several or many topics. Thus consideration of flexibility, for example, must surely take account, not only of individual items of accommodation but also of how they are associated with one another and the plan form which results from this association.

118. The Maiden Erlegh exercise demonstrates the concept of flexibility which not only permits of day-to-day change in the teaching/learning programme, in the variety and type of educational activities and in the sizes of working groups—in fact, its first aim—but can also accommodate considerable changes in function solely by the relocation of furniture, movable storage units and screens. What enables these changes is essentially the provision of a large general or non-committed teaching space, punctuated or articulated by specialised or committed spaces. Separate specialised blocks of accommodation would hardly be likely to give this flexibility which can only come about where the units of accommodation are large enough and have sufficient diversity of accommodation to house a variety of facilities and thus to offer a range of choices of learning possibilities.

119. And yet there are limits to this flexibility. The final two plans in the Maiden Erlegh exercise give examples of where these limits are overstepped—some removal and addition of internal walls is involved in one example, and in the other, the extension of existing services is required. Adaptability thus takes over from flexibility when the limits of flexibility are reached. Nevertheless, the exercise clearly demonstrates that where flexibility is provided in the form of a continuum of activity zones, of non-committed and committed spaces then the need for, and the problems of, adaptability become less acute.

120. Even if a building is planned as a continuum of activity zones, it will certainly include some defined or wall-bounded areas first, for those specialised or committed teaching spaces that house activities that require them (for example, activities requiring sound insulation or privacy) and secondly, for staircases, lavatories or areas that need fire protection. Some areas, whether enclosed or "open" may require direct access and association with external courts or yards which may themselves be used for teaching purposes and which the building can usefully protect and shelter.

121. The Sucy-en-Brie case example illustrates some of the features of such a plan form. In the design of this building those areas intended for use for technical and scientific work were isolated; there was a separation of "fixed" (stairs, lavatories, main vertical service runs) and "adaptable" (non-committed) general accommodation, and the dimensioning of the building to avoid complex lighting and ventilation problems.

122. The crucial importance of this dimensioning of the building can be understood by contrasting the design exercises on Sucy-en-Brie and Arlington respectively. The former plan form accommodated the hypothetical model with comparative ease, whereas that of the latter presented certain marked difficulties on account of the greater depth of the building. The principal difficulties stem not only from the requirement in the exercise to naturally light teaching space or at least give a "view-out" (see "Design Decisions or Assumptions" paragraph 24)—a requirement which may to some be of questionable validity—but also from the sheer numbers of people and their disposition in the deep plan and, more importantly, the rigidity of the circulation patterns set up by these numbers and this depth. Where the plan form comprises units of accommodation which are less deep and cater for smaller numbers of people then problems of logistics do not assume such importance.

123. Yet it has been shown that units of accommodation must be "large enough and

have sufficient diversity of accommodation to house a variety of facilities" (paragraph 118). So, what is "large enough"; what depth of plan will give such units? It is impossible from the work undertaken during this study to be precise about dimensions—to be so would require further more specific work on the subject. But it is clear that too small a dimension could not give sufficient diversity of accommodation whereas too large a dimension leads to a loss of flexibility. Present indications, however, emphasise the importance of adopting a plan form which offers a continuity of space within and between units of accommodation and seem to cast doubt on plan depths over 21 metres.

124. A further important factor affecting plan depth and the ability of a building to accommodate change is the number of storeys. The problems or constraints associated with a multi-storey building are undoubtedly greater than those met with one storey. First, there is the question of light penetration into, and ventilation of, a deep plan: both purposes are infinitely more easy to serve in single storey buildings by the simple expedient of puncturing the roof—to provide roof lights, natural ventilators, even courtyards. Second, a single-storey offers greater freedom in the location of specialised facilities which involve special equipment with special servicing requirements or unusual weight (take, for example, a forge): in a multi-storey building the positioning of such facilities is constrained by the need to group them round shared vertical service ducts or runs which, in turn, have repercussions on each floor as they rise through the building. Third, the demands of circulation to, from and between facilities are more difficult to satisfy and more space-consuming in buildings of more than one storey in which the number of main circulation nodes necessarily equals the number of staircases with the consequent, almost inevitable, setting up of powerful "traffic" routes between them: in a single-storey building, circulation is not so restricted and traffic can be more easily dispersed and managed.

125. This is not to say that all school building should be restricted to one storey. Clearly, the consequences of doing so on the sizes of school sites needed would, in many cases, have unthinkable financial implications. Nevertheless, the aim should surely be to limit the number of storeys as far as possible and, just as importantly, closely to consider how much and what parts of the school can be disposed on more than one storey without giving rise to the problems raised above—or, at least, to minimise these problems. For example, accommodation which does not possess special requirements in terms of, say, heavy equipment or a high degree of servicing might well be disposed over several storeys without the layout of one storey dictating or, in some measure, determining that of those above or below. Likewise, "blocks" of accommodation which can operate in a largely self-contained way may be so disposed, one on top of the other, so that the day-to-day operation of each is, to a great extent, independant of the others thus minimising traffic flows between and through them and reducing mutual interference and space committed to mere circulation.

126. These then are the factors which govern the plan form and depth and relative disposition or location of the elements and installations that make up this plan form in order to arrive at a building which offers possibilities for day-to-day change in its use. They are also the factors which underlie the provision of adaptability to meet longer term, more radical, change for it is clear that whatever is located in the first instance in a building —whenever and however—it affects a great many other things; and since adaptability is a good deal more demanding than mere internal spatial variation (see paragraph 109) and, in practice, involves replacement, removal and/or addition of, for instance, fittings, equipment, finishes and services (though in this last case removal is unlikely save in the most exceptional cases), the elements of the plan form and its installations should be located in such a way as to permit such replacement, removal and/or addition with minimal effect on, or disruption to, other such elements or installations.

LOCATION AND SITING

127. It has been stated earlier in this report that new school buildings need to be considered as additions to the existing stock of buildings and need looking at not in isolation but in relation to other built facilities existing or proposed in their locality (paragraph 94). The central importance of determining or framing the school network in such consideration is self-evident as is the need for careful analysis of the existing stock of schools and buildings which might serve school purposes. The analysis should indicate, in addition to the location, size or capacity of facilities, the age and condition of the buildings, their needs in terms of educational or purely physical updating and their potential for use for whatever other purposes—educational or community—

which may, at some time, be considered appropriate or desirable. There are indications that changes in the functions of buildings, or parts of buildings, will become increasingly important in the future if efficient use is to be made of available resources.

128. Such changes in use, or joint or shared use do not, of course, represent a radically new concept: schools and evening institutes, for example, have cohabited for many years. What is new is the scale and degree of sharing or joint use envisaged and the nature of the relationships of formerly separate facilities one to the other and to their wider urban, suburban or rural context. Projects already realised and at present under active consideration in Member countries of the OECD include small rural schools designed to serve dispersed populations and providing facilities for local community and recreational activities, single buildings in which a number of functions and organisations are accommodated under one roof, dispersed facilities managed and used in a co-ordinated manner, and "campus" schemes in which facilities are grouped together by function or organisation in a number of separate buildings on the same site or in the same locality.

129. The objectives of such projects are various, the problems they pose considerable,

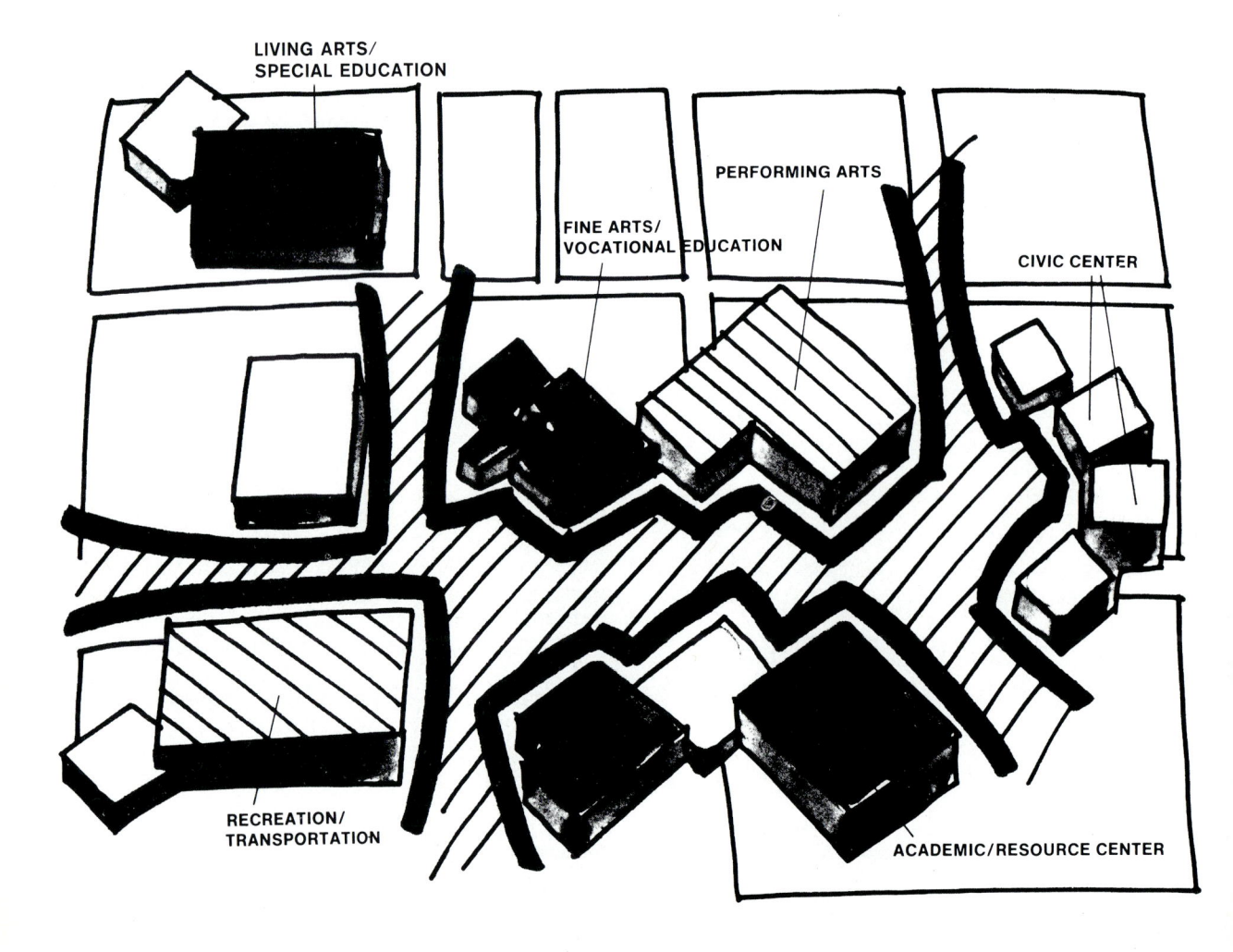

Figure 16: **A theoretical proposal for a "dispersed site system", considered as a network of resources and services, with facilities managed and used in a co-ordinated manner.**

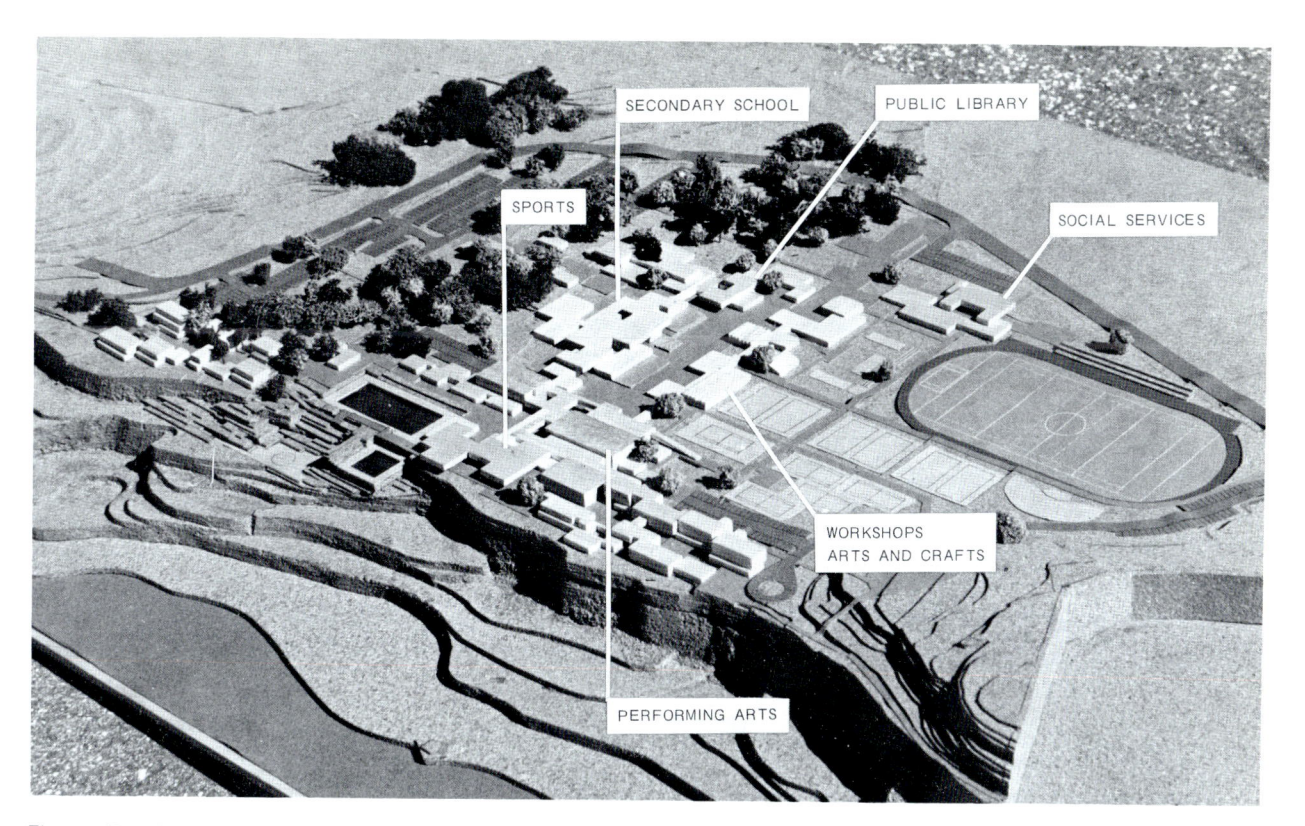

Figure 17: **An example of a "campus" solution, recently built and in which the facilities are grouped together by function in a number of separate buildings on the same site.**

and the benefits they bring as yet arguable and insufficiently proved. The OECD Programme on Educational Building, recognising the increasing attention which the topic is engaging, is undertaking a two-year study entitled "Co-ordination of School and Community Facilities" with the broad objective of bringing together recent international experience in this field, analysing the various approaches adopted towards solving the problems posed and clarifying the policy issues involved. Without prejudging the outcome of this study, it is expected that some light will be thrown on whether, and how, a co-ordinated approach to organisation, planning and management not only leads to a better use of resources and extends educational and socio-cultural opportunities but also—and this is a direct concern of the present study—makes a significant contribution to coping with the problems set by educational and social change.

130. Intimately connected with the question of location of facilities is that of site availability. Oblique reference has already been made to this problem earlier when discussing the number of storeys of a building and its effect on flexibility and adaptability (paragraph 125). And implicit in this reference was a conflict between the need to limit the number of storeys and the prohibitive cost of acquiring large sites in many cases—particularly in urban growth areas where demand for land for all purposes is at its highest.

131. But the desire to limit the number of storeys is not the only pressure for large school sites: the needs of the future may well demand extensions to existing buildings or additional new accommodation in close proximity—needs which can be met by the initial provision of a site area surplus to immediate

requirements. Likewise, high land costs are not the only factor militating against the provision of large sites: the isolation of school buildings from their urban setting by excessive open spaces could well run counter to educational or social aims which seek to co-ordinate more closely school and community interests and activities—aims which might be better met by a closer physical integration of their respective facilities.

Figure 18: **Isolation of a school from its urban setting makes difficult the closer co-ordination with the community which is one of the social aims pursued by this school.**

132. Architectural, educational, financial, social and town-planning considerations enter into these questions of location, siting and inter-relationship of built facilities as well as consideration of the implications of future change. And what seems certain is that the right answer to these questions is most likely to result not from the pursuit of one of these considerations to the exclusion of the rest, but only if all are held in some way in balance. Such a balance is unlikely to be susceptible to any kind of golden rule but, as far as the concerns of this study go, it is safe to say that the initial provision of facilities in a way that does not completely exploit or commit the sites they occupy to specific or exclusive uses will go a long way towards easing the problems of future growth or change.

ENVIRONMENT AND SERVICES

133. The dangers of concentrating on the relocatability of partitions have been discussed and its consequences for other elements or attributes of the building touched on. Among these consequences, the effect on the internal environment of the school is perhaps the most significant. Take, for example, the artificial lighting and its control by switches by the door; or recall the effect on the natural lighting distribution if a room is narrowed in relation to its width, or the possible effects on ventilation. In some attempts to provide partition relocatability these factors have been largely ignored.

134. In cases where they have been recognised, and measures taken to deal with them, relocatability of partitions has necessitated corresponding relocatability of all the elements —lighting, switch controls, ventilation inlets and so on—that are associated with them, and costs have risen in proportion. Furthermore, the difficulties of relocation have been reduced by ensuring that floors and ceilings can remain unchanged; this has attracted architects to provide a uniform floor and ceiling finish throughout the building. And, in order to avoid the difficulties associated with lighting —natural and artificial—it has tempted them to seek, with debatable justification, a totally artificial internal environment, which further raises costs and, still more seriously, denies to schools the educational advantage of contact with or awareness of the outside world.

135. All these effects lead to the uniformity in every aspect of the school environment referred to earlier (paragraph 111)—the adaptability where it is least required and no adaptability where it is really needed. Yet, even though the inherent limitations of relocatability —first of partitions and consequently of practically all other elements of the building—are thus demonstrated, the concept of adaptability is in no way destroyed. For there is still no denying that there are limits to flexibility and that buildings over their lifetime need physical alteration to meet the changed requirements of the users.

136. But it is essential to recognise two facts. First, that the size and shapes of rooms and the relationships between them are not of sole or even paramount importance, the other environmental factors such as lighting, ventilation, heating (and the services necessary to them), acoustics and tactile finishes being equally if not much more of concern as well as the services directly required for teaching purposes—water, drainage, electricity and gas supply, etc. Secondly, paying more in first cost for uncertain benefits in the future represents an investment which may possibly bring

Figure 19: **A totally artificial environment may lead to lack of contact with or awareness of the outside world.**

no return; in short, adaptability is best obtainable without extra first total cost—an aspect to which the report returns later under the heading "Cost Considerations". And this first cost needs to be measured not just in financial terms but also in terms of any sacrifice of immediate convenience. It is hard to justify meeting the unknowable needs of the future where it is at the expense of the known needs of today.

137. In the light of these two facts a strategy for maximising provision for change without excessive first costs or sacrifice of present needs can be discerned. In essence this strategy may be summed up as resting on a policy of "pay-as-you-go" rather than of "pay-in-advance". To spend money on maximising the relocatability of any component in the building is to pay in advance. To defer expenditure until adaptation is actually needed is to pay as you go. The strategy is to design what is needed in the present in such a way that, without incurring excessive first cost, expenditure on subsequent adaptation will not be increased by the nature of the initial provision.

138. Aspects of what this implies in practice have been dealt with elsewhere—for example, an overall plan form giving blocks of accommodation the layout of which comprises a judicious mix of basic and specialised workplaces permitting the early conversion of basic into specialised or vice-versa rather than one kind of specialised into another. Similar considerations apply as far as environment and services are concerned. Here again, undue emphasis on relocation is misplaced. For, as the case examples show, relocation is less important to adaptation than replacement, removal or addition.

139. The creation of the right thermal conditions, for example, often relies on installations and service runs which, by the very nature of the task they have to perform, are fairly evenly distributed throughout the building. Nevertheless, the manner of their distribution is subject to the discretion of the designers and the aim should be to dispose them in a way that first, does not militate against the flexible use of space by, for instance, obtruding into the continuum of space provided (and discussed earlier) and second, permits of replacement, removal and/or addition with minimal effect to other elements or installations in the building. Two questions then are important: where to locate the installations and their services and, equally important, what to fix them to.

140. The same questions apply to the fulfilment of other needs that involve installations and services whether for environmental or for teaching purposes. Lighting, ventilation, plumbing, drainage—all demand that the problems of location and fixing be considered at the outset to safeguard the ability of the building to accommodate change. A lack of the necessary services, or their provision without regard to possible future demands in terms of changed temperature, lighting, air supply or teaching equipment requirements can render a building unresponsive to educational change other than at unreasonable or prohibitive cost.

141. And yet, as has been shown, too technologically sophisticated an answer to these questions can also lead to unreasonable costs (but this time first costs rather than subsequent costs of adaptation) and run counter to the very objectives it is sought to promote by resulting in a patent mismatch between other aspects of the environment—for instance, acoustic or aural characteristics and surface finishes (floors, walls, ceilings)—and the activities that they should facilitate. In the course of the visits made under this study, many cases were found where teachers were obliged to cover universal carpeting with untidy plastic sheeting in order to carry out wet or messy activities which would spoil the carpet.

142. All the foregoing evidence points to the need for buildings in which some elements are permanent and unchanging and in which other elements can be added, removed or replaced as and when the need arises. Here the use of structural frames rather than load-bearing walls is an obvious starting point. But it is no more than a starting point which warrants further consideration in relation to the incorporation of services and subsequent additions to them.

STRUCTURE

143. That a structural frame is an obvious starting point in providing for change is demonstrated by the design exercises. It allows easy re-arrangement of furniture and equipment to create appropriate facilities for different teaching/learning situations; it permits easy addition, removal or replacement of partitions; and it presents fewer obstacles to the installation of new services which may be required to create new environmental conditions—for example, higher intensity of lighting, increased ventilation; or to serve new teaching equipment—for example, water supply, drainage.

144. The design exercises also suggest that uneconomically long floor or roof spans are less important than hitherto supposed. One of the exercises shows quite clearly that the most extreme educational change imaginable can be almost entirely accommodated within a column spacing of 7.20 metres in both directions. That the change cannot be wholly accommodated is due to the fact that a drama area is obstructed by a column, and that no unobstructed space can be found large enough for physical education purposes.

145. The difficulties encountered in the exercise just described underline, if any underlining is needed, the undeniable necessity in the modern school for diversity of accommodation, previously discussed, and suggest that the "optimum grid" for the structural frame—a grid which can accommodate all the spaces which may be required—is a chimera. What is needed is a less regular grid that offers variation or choice in structural spans and can thus provide for the diversity required.

146. A grid which gives the option of closer column spacing in one direction, for instance, can be quite acceptable if it gives a long one in the other. Such a grid would have enabled the drama area described above (paragraph 144) to be freed of its obstructive column by ranging the close-spaced columns on the line of the boundary walls of the area and allowing the long spans at right angles to provide a clear span over the area. Of course, a uniform or regular large span of, say, 14 metres in both directions would also have given an alternative way of avoiding the obstructive column in question but only at the expense of providing large spans where they are unlikely ever to be used: the Arlington exercise clearly shows that where such a large span grid is adopted very little is gained in terms of ease of adaptability as far as most of the accommodation is concerned.

147. A further advantage of using a column grid that makes possible spans no larger than they need be over an important part of the building is that the increments of accommodation that can be added to the building—both in the first instance and in connection with subsequent adaptations or extensions—are smaller and thus easier to tailor to actual needs. There is little to be gained by providing large increments of accommodation on account of large spans where they are unlikely to be fully used owing to their excessive size or their inappropriate location.

148. Under the previous heading it was noted that the structural frame "...warrants consideration in relation to the incorporation of services..." (paragraph 142) and, previous to that, that two questions are of particular importance, namely "...where to locate the installations and their service runs and, equally important, what to fix them to" (paragraph 139). Two locations and fixing elements immediately suggest themselves by virtue of their unobstrusive and in all likelihood, their permanent and unchanging nature: the perimeter walls (other than where specific provision is initially made for future extension) and ceilings or undersides of floors and roofs. Yet both these locations need particular consideration from the point of view of structure if easy incorporation of services is to be ensured.

149. Perimeter locations and fixings are difficult with certain types of frame which depend on the thickening or strengthening of structural edge-members for structural stability or which include wind-bracing elements which already occupy these locations. In both instances, the passage of vertical service runs is restricted and either these restrictions need to be minimised by a design which permits the removal of those parts which prevent such passage or an alternative structure chosen which solves the problems of stability and wind-bracing in another way. Likewise with floor- or roof-located service runs: a structure which enables the removal of floor or roof panels (as, for example, with certain types of precast unit construction) or the puncturing of the floor or roof (for example, a waffle slab) offers considerable advantage over the continuous slab.

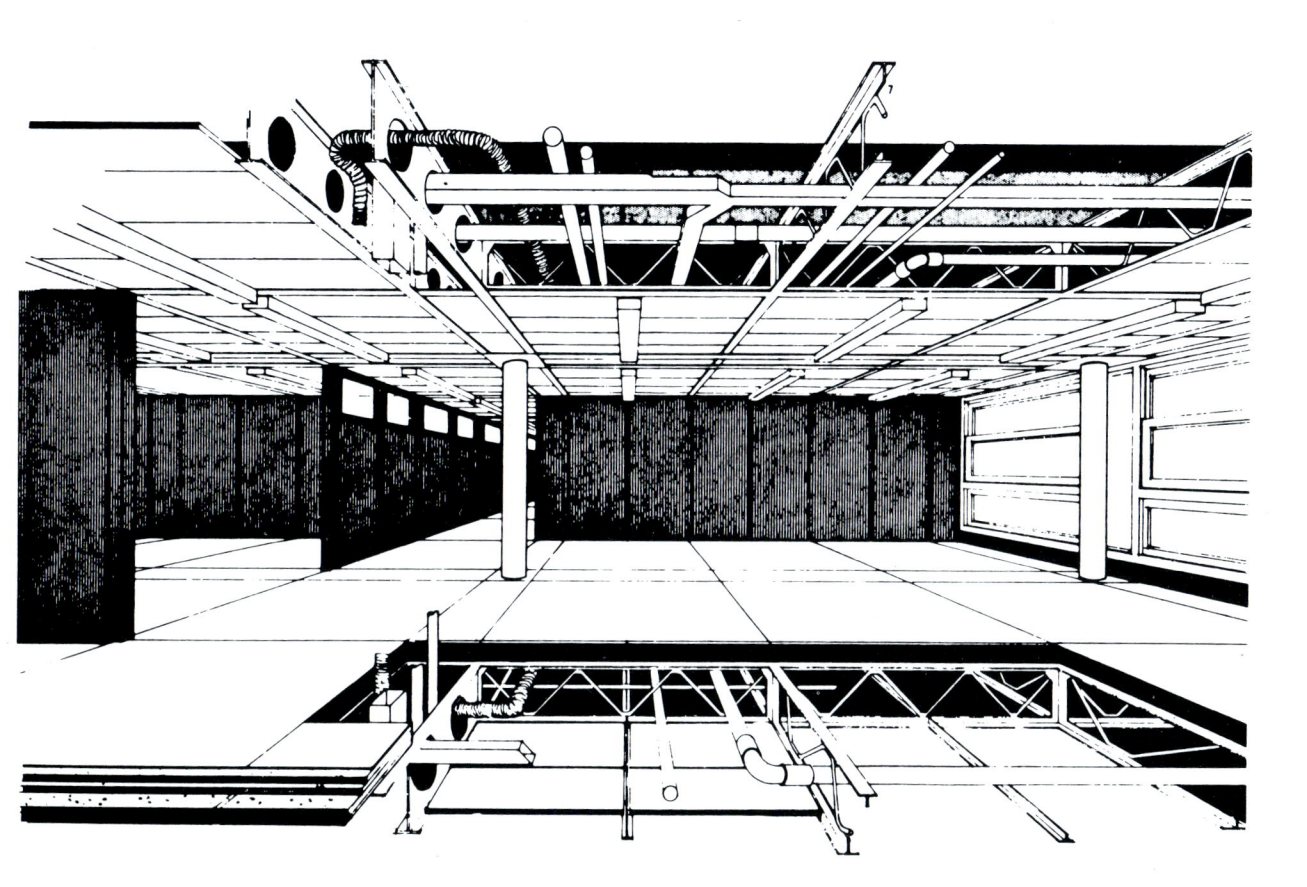

Figure 20: **A floor or roof structure which allows the easy incorporation of new horizontal service runs, an important feature of adaptability.**

150. Where the floor or roof structure is composite—for example, steel beams carrying precast concrete decking—the incorporation of new horizontal service runs or equipment can be easily accomplished using lattice girders or castellated beams. Both Maiden Erlegh and Arlington are examples of this sort of construction: the services simply occupy the space between the underside of the floor or roof and the underside of the supporting beams; a suspended ceiling may or may not be provided at the lower of these levels depending on whether it is sought to conceal the services or, perhaps, to provide a sound-absorbing surface for acoustic purposes. Where the structure is homogeneous—for example, a concrete slab with supporting downstand concrete beams or a two-way waffle slab—the penetration of horizontal service runs or accommodation of ceiling-mounted equipment is not as easily accomplished and floor-to-ceiling heights should be such as to allow subsequent mounting of such services and equipment (or sound-absorbing surfaces) without making the headroom insufficient. An example of such construction is given by Sucy-en-Brie.

151. From these considerations, three key points emerge as being central to the capacity of the structure to cope with change: first, the extent to which any part of the structure is removable (without, needless to say, interfering with structural stability or wind-bracing); second, the ability to penetrate the structure, whether steel, concrete, fibreglass; and third, the amount of clearance around the structure (which does not overlap with space which is already committed to, for example, providing necessary headroom).

FURNITURE AND EQUIPMENT

152. There can be no doubt that the quickest response to change and one of the major contributions to the easy accommodation of new uses in a building comes from furniture and equipment. The replacement of tip-up seat/desk combinations by easily portable and stackable chairs and tables, for instance, has helped considerably in the change from teacher-centred to child-centred activity. Many innovations are marked by the introduction of some new piece of equipment. The more portable the equipment and furniture and the more easily it can be stored and stacked, the greater the range of activities which can go on in the space in which it is used.

153. The important role played by movable furniture and equipment in maximising flexibility is clear, allowing teachers and pupils to re-arrange their accommodation when the need arises. Some have recognised this and have sought to increase this flexibility by mobilising, often with considerable ingenuity and inventiveness, items which are normally fixed (for example, sinks, storage, display) and, furthermore, seeing such mobility as a means whereby teachers can sub-divide space exactly to their liking without the need for partitions (thus missing most of its point), they have provided the largest possible undivided (and, of course, uniform) space. Enough has been said previously of the dangers of this uniformity; it is repeated here merely to show that treating the mobilisation of furniture and equipment as an article of faith and employing it to serve the ends of variable space sub-division can ultimately be self-defeating.

154. Just as many educational activities may need a particular environment or have particular spatial requirements so they may need particular furniture and equipment. Indeed, many activities are generally described in terms of the equipment used—for example welding or forging. And just as workplaces can be split into basic and specialised, and spaces into non-committed and committed, so can furniture and equipment needs be split. These splits raise again the question of workplace and space specialisation.

155. If a space is devoted permanently to the use of one type of special furniture or

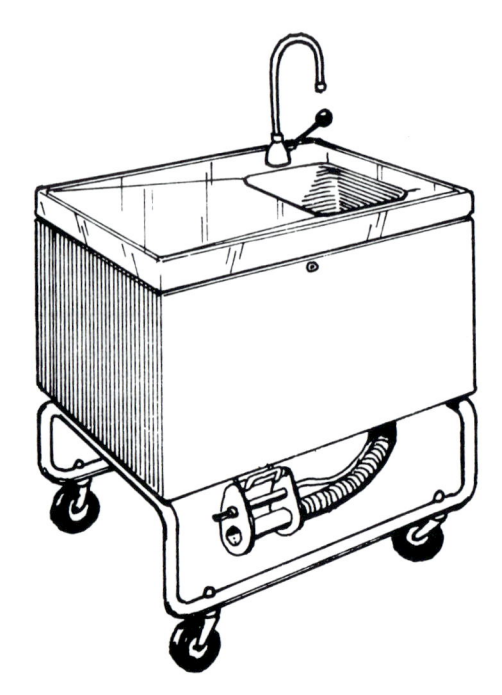

Figure 21: **A mobile sink facilitates the flexible use of space and minimises the need for committing space.**

Figure 22: **Compact and light audio-visual equipment can provide temporary specialised workplaces in a general teaching area.**

piece of equipment, it inevitably dictates group size in relation to a particular teaching function; it becomes, in fact, a committed space and forms a rigid feature which can militate against flexible use of that part of the school that it occupies. With the use of mobile forms of furniture and equipment however, such commitment of space can be reduced and the degree to which the school building needs to be designed to the requirements of particular items of furniture and equipment can be minimised—thus increasing flexibility in use.

156. This then is the way to look at the mobilisation of furniture and equipment—and not, as many architects have done, as a way of sub-dividing spaces. Daylight projection equipment, re-chargeable power-packs, simple and cheap recording facilities, transistorised television monitors, compact and relatively light audio-visual equipment: all these can be deployed whenever and wherever the teaching demands it without being tied down by, or dependent on, the building and building services.

COST CONSIDERATIONS

157. Providing for future change—whether it is aimed for through flexibility or through adaptability—inevitably has consequences for the cost of school building. In both cases, a single-minded pursuit of maximising such provision can lead to exceptionally high costs. And in both cases it is clear that a satisfactory balance needs to be struck between aims and costs. Moreover, it seems improbable that such a balance can be struck unless there is clear indication of what maximum cost is acceptable.

158. In the case of flexibility, the consequences are reflected in the initial cost of adopting some of the measures needed to maximise flexibility. For example, increasing the range of facilities in, or associated with, any item of accommodation to permit greater variation of activity pattern; or providing an excess of the real number of workplaces for an activity over the theoretical number of pupils engaged on it—both inevitably increase the cost. On the other hand, the provision of large general or non-committed spaces punctuated or articulated by specialised or committed spaces may be realised in such a way as to almost totally eliminate the specific and exclusive function of circulation over an important part of a building—this represents a saving in cost.

159. It is by setting such increases in cost against such savings in cost that expenditure on flexibility can be kept in check. All the factors that lead to flexibility should be so evaluated from the decisions on spatial layout and plan form to the choice of furniture and equipment—the important contribution that well-chosen mobile furniture and storage units can make has been discussed under the previous heading. Thus, in assessing the cost of flexibility the total cost equation for the school should be established and the balance between increases and savings, between building costs and furniture and equipment costs determined.

160. As far as adaptability is concerned, costs need consideration under two heads: the cost of adaptability itself; and the subsequent cost of adaptation if and when it is required. Cost of adaptability is, of course, a first cost and represents an investment made in the expectation or hope of a future benefit. The future benefit is adaptation costing sufficiently less than it would without the investment. Considered in financial terms, the future cost saving must be discounted to represent its present value, which in turn must be greater than the cost of adaptability if the adaptability is to be worth buying.

161. To estimate the financial cost of future adaptation and convert it to present values demands, however, an element of guesswork concerning the magnitude and frequency of adaptation, how far into the future each adaptation will occur, and what discounting rate should be used in the calculation. Furthermore, it must be recognised that future benefits are at best arguable, whereas immediate first costs of adaptability, if incurred, are an inescapable reality. Take, for example, an initial investment in total relocatability of partitioning: the design exercises show how, in fact, no more than a small proportion of partitions is likely to need relocation. Suppose the proportion is as high as 20 per cent and the extra cost for relocatability per unit of partition is 10 per cent (even without the extra cost of associated elements—see paragraph 162—this would be remarkably low) then the real cost of the relocated elements is 50 per cent higher.

162. Indirect as well as direct costs of adaptability need to be noted. For example, if a partition which is relocatable costs no more than one which is not, there is no direct cost, but if, in order to allow for relocation, the beams of floors or roofs above the partitions need to span a greater distance, then the consequent extra is an indirect cost of partition relocatability. If, in the interests of partition relocatability, switches and power outlets normally fixed to partitions have to be located in less convenient positions this again is an indirect cost on which some value should be placed. Likewise, in considering costs of adaptation: attention is needed to the cost or estimated cost of the operation not only in terms of finance but also of skill required and disruption caused to normal activity.

163. All adaptability which depends on the demounting and replacement of building elements or components poses a serious problem which, in turn, leads to an important and fundamental question. The problem is the storage of components that are not immediately required—where they are to be kept, their likely deterioration and possible obsolescence. And the question is, is it worth considering their provision in the first place in case they might be needed later? Or is it better to wait and see what is required when the need for change actually occurs? Answers to these questions will depend on the particular circumstances of each case as will the decisions taken concerning the balance between first costs of adaptability and future costs of adaptation.

164. The provision of flexibility and of adaptability, it can be seen, has complex cost implications involving in each case the balancing of immediate and expected benefits and expenditure. Neither of these can be accurately weighed in totally scientific terms, the first owing to the necessarily subjective judgement involved, and both on account of the inevitably unpredictable turn of future events. But in this they are no different from other aspects of architectural design: a successful building will always rely on the experience and judgement of its designers in balancing the competing claims put forward. Thus providing flexibility and adaptability should be considered as yet one more of the numerous desiderata that it is within the discretion of the designers to weigh and balance. Concentration on any one of these desiderata will inevitably be at the expense of one or more of the others so an important first design task must be to establish priorities.

165. The establishment of these priorities and the whole process of briefing and design is undoubtedly aided by a prior indication of the level of permissible expenditure. Where this level is indirectly limited by a ceiling imposed on quantitative and qualitative standards—for example, in the form of prescribed floor areas—the necessary discretion is denied to designers and educational or technological innovation greatly inhibited. With direct expenditure norms no such denial or inhibitions are involved but instead a positive stimulus which enables building designers to consider the desirable in the light of the possible, thus compelling the making of choices.

Part Four
SUMMARY OF CONCLUSIONS

166. Emerging from the not inconsiderable work that has gone into the carrying out of this study, and in particular the design exercises on which much of it is based, are important conclusions which can be expressed in the form of a number of strategy pointers. These concern a wide range of policy and implementation issues in many fields. They are naturally closely interrelated but are set out below under various heads corresponding to the areas in which they have their major impact.

Education

167. The nature of provision needed to facilitate future change depends on and varies with the nature of the provision made to meet the needs of the present. Whatever provision is made for future change should not be at the expense of sacrificing present educational needs.

168. Variation in enrolment numbers coupled with a wider range of curriculum options always demands an excess of workplaces over pupil places. The more advanced the trend in this direction the greater the flexibility of the resulting building and the later the point where adaptation will be needed. If, on the other hand, present needs call for only a restricted range of accommodation or facilities the need for adaptation is likely to occur sooner than if the needs and range are wide.

169. If educational policy imposes rigid patterns of daily activity on the school, adaptation is likely to be needed sooner than if the school enjoys some freedom and autonomy in its curricular arrangements which allow it to adapt those to the facilities available.

170. Likewise, excessive precision in educational demands (in terms of prescribed floor areas, numbers and disposition of teaching spaces, etc.) will surely lead to the need for adaptation earlier than if variation of accommodation is permitted and architects can more freely interpret the wishes of their clients. This necessitates a design team with educationists appointed to voice educational requirements and to safeguard educational interests and objectives.

Management

171. The attitudes of individuals and organisations—their ability, capacity or, indeed, willingness to themselves adapt in exploiting opportunities for change within a building through organisation, management and use of the facilities offered—are of critical importance. The potential of individuals to adapt themselves to environmental circumstances needs encouragement rather than resistance on the part of the authorities to which they are responsible.

172. Much useful change can be accommodated at minor cost by improvisations made by teachers or by the substitution or introduction of more suitable furniture and equipment. Easy access of teachers to the authority and willingness of the authority to provide modest financial assistance in response are however essential if advantage is to be taken of this possibility.

Finance and Planning

173. Nothing in the study supports the view that higher initial cost is justified to provide for meeting unforeseeable future change. Much more valuable is careful consideration of where and how in the building the available money is spent. The use of structural frames instead of load-bearing walls is one obvious example of a number of technological devices which can be used to increase adaptability in new buildings without increasing first cost.

174. But if subsequent advantage is to be taken of the opportunities such devices offer, finance must be made available for adaptation when it is required. This strategy can be summed up, quite simply, as "pay-as-you-go" rather than "pay-in-advance".

175. Sites which permit some expansion of facilities should it be required are an aid to this strategy and, consequently, careful consideration of the relative location of school and other community facilities is called for; when change occurs, the possibility of reaching the new balance of facilities required by looking beyond the school premises then presents itself.

Technology

176. The use of a structural frame rather than load-bearing walls goes a long way towards easing the problems set by future change. But uniformly long floor or roof spans contribute little to adaptability and can prove expensive, diverting resources away from where they are really needed. More important is to adopt a structural frame which offers the possibility of a range of spans or structural layouts in order to match the diversity of accommodation which, in practice, is what is needed.

177. Likewise, total relocatability of partitions represents an investment which brings little or no return and which, furthermore, militates against achieving this necessary diversity of accommodation.

178. Adaptability is best sought in the fields directly affecting variety of environment and supplies of electricity, water and drainage. But here, as with partitions, relocation is less important than the facility to add, replace or remove. In practice, this means a structure which enables some removal or puncturing of building elements in order to ease installation of extra services and/or the provision of adequate headroom, or clearance around building elements, to accommodate such installation.

Design

179. As far as is consistent with meeting the needs of the present, greatest emphasis should be placed on maximising flexibility. There is no reason to suppose that the measures required to secure this flexibility need extra expenditure. Rather they will involve re-allocation of the resources already made available and depend on the skill and judgement of the designers.

180. The aim should be to provide an excess of workplaces over the number of occupants; to widen the range of activities which general space can accommodate by means of, for example, mobile furniture and equipment; to widen the range of specialised workplaces in order to widen the range of opportunity; to optimise the proportion of general to committed space and to provide for easy conversion of specialised workplaces into basic workplaces or vice-versa rather than one kind of specialised into another.

181. These measures, in turn, imply a plan form which permits a continuum of activity zones punctuated or articulated with committed spaces and which is so dimensioned as to avoid complex lighting, ventilation and circulation problems.

182. Adaptability, to facilitate adaptation if and when it is required, is further enhanced by providing as much of the accommodation as possible in single-storey buildings and by leaving space on the site for future extensions.

183. Finally, it should be recorded that, despite the effort put into this study, the topic of providing for future change is undoubtedly one which warrants yet further attention by national authorities with a view to making the conclusions more specific to their particular circumstances. It is strongly recommended that national study teams carry out the kind of design exercises that are detailed in Part Two of this report as a basis for subsequent development work in which the findings are given practical application.

ACKNOWLEDGEMENTS

Sources for the plans, figures and tables related to the case-studies are as follows:

MAIDEN ERLEGH

Project	Maiden Erlegh Secondary School, Earley, United Kingdom.
Architects	The Development Group, the Architects and Building Branch, Department of Education and Science, London.
Plan 1	From **Building Bulletin 48,** HMSO, London, reproduced with the permission of the Controller of Her Britannic Majesty's Stationery Office, London.
Plans 2 to 6	Prepared by the team in charge of the study at the offices of the Ellis/Williams Partnership, Manchester.

SUCY-EN-BRIE

Project	Collège d'Enseignement Secondaire, Quartier du Fort, Sucy-en-Brie, France.
Architects	Robert Joly, Groupement d'Architectes, Paris.
Plans 7 to 10	Redrawn to scale after the original working drawings provided by the architects.
Plans 11 to 14	Prepared by the team in charge of the study at the offices at Ellis/Williams Partnership, Manchester.

ARLINGTON

Project	Arlington Senior Public School, York, Canada.
Architects	Brook, Carruthers, Grierson, Shaw, Toronto, Ontario.
Plans 15 to 17	Redrawn to scale after the original working drawings provided by the architects through the Director of Education for the Borough of York.
Plans 18 to 20	Prepared by the team in charge of the study at the offices of the Ellis/Williams Partnership, Manchester.

Figures 1 to 6 and Tables 1 to 10 are the responsibility of the team in charge of the study.

Sources for the following figures are as follows:

7. Plan of Brize Norton Primary School, Oxfordshire, reproduced from Eric Pearson, **Trends in School Design,** Macmillan Education Ltd., London, 1972, with the permission of the Schools Council Publications 1972.

10. Project — Delf Hill Middle School, Bradford.
    Architects — Bradford Architects Department in association with the Development Group of the Architects and Building Branch of the Department of Education and Science, London.
    Photograph — Provided by the Architects and Building Branch and reproduced with the permission of the Controller of Her Britannic Majesty's Stationery Office, London.

14. Plan drawn from **International School Building News,** 7/1973/No. 1, "Development project low-cost comprehensive school in Lelystad, the Netherlands", prepared by the Information Centre for School Building and published by the Bouwcentrum, Rotterdam.

15. Project — St. Thomas of Canterbury RC Primary School.
    Architects — The Ellis/Williams Partnership, Manchester.
    Plan — Provided by the architects.

16. From **Community/School: Sharing the Space and the Action,** Educational Facilities Laboratories, Inc., New York, 1973.

17. Project — Centre Educatif et Culturel, Istres, France.
    Architects — Riboulet, Thurnauer and Véret; architect in charge: Faure-Ladreyt.
    Photograph — Provided by the architects.

20. From an English brochure on the **CROCS School Building System** provided by the architects of the system: Cahen, Dumas, Valloton, Weber, Busset, Lyon, Réalisations scolaires et sportives, Lausanne-Chailly, Switzerland.

21. From the catalogue of the **ff5 School Casework System** of Cameron McIndoo, Don Mills, Ontario, Canada.

The following figures belong to the PEB Secretariat, OECD, Paris:

8. Project — Marton Church of England Primary School.
   Architects — Design Group Partnership; architect in charge: N.T. Evans.

9,10. Project — Pleasant View, Willowdale, Ontario, Canada.
      Architects — Boigon and Heinonen.

12. Project — Gorsthill County Junior School, Ellesmere Port, Cheshire.
    Architects — Cheshire County Council Architects Department.

13. Project — Rannebergen Infant School, Göteborg, Sweden.
    Architects — White AB.

18. Project — Integrierte Gesamtschule, Fröndenberg, Germany.
    Architects — Dipl. Ing. Jan Bassenge MA.
    Dipl. Ing. Kay Pyhan-Schultz.
    Dipl. Ing. Hasso F. Schreck.
    Architektengemeinschaft, Berlin.

19,22. Project — Arlington Senior Public School, York, Canada.
       Architects — Brook, Carruthers, Grierson, Shaw, Toronto, Ontario.

OECD SALES AGENTS
DEPOSITAIRES DES PUBLICATIONS DE L'OCDE

ARGENTINA – ARGENTINE
Carlos Hirsch S.R.L.,
Florida 165, BUENOS-AIRES.
☎ 33-1787-2391 Y 30-7122
AUSTRALIA – AUSTRALIE
International B.C.N. Library Suppliers Pty Ltd.,
161 Sturt St., South MELBOURNE, Vic. 3205.
☎ 69.7601
658 Pittwater Road, BROOKVALE NSW 2100.
☎ 938 2267
AUSTRIA – AUTRICHE
Gerold and Co., Graben 31, WIEN 1.
☎ 52.22.35
BELGIUM – BELGIQUE
Librairie des Sciences
Coudenberg 76-78, B 1000 BRUXELLES 1.
☎ 512-05-60
BRAZIL – BRESIL
Mestre Jou S.A., Rua Guaipá 518,
Caixa Postal 24090, 05089 SAO PAULO 10.
☎ 256-2746/262-1609
Rua Senador Dantas 19 s/205-6, RIO DE JANEIRO GB. ☎ 232-07. 32
CANADA
Information Canada
171 Slater, OTTAWA. KIA 0S9.
☎ (613) 992-9738
DENMARK – DANEMARK
Munksgaards Boghandel
Nørregade 6, 1165 KØBENHAVN K.
☎ (01) 12 69 70
FINLAND – FINLANDE
Akateeminen Kirjakauppa
Keskuskatu 1, 00100 HELSINKI 10. ☎ 625.901
FRANCE
Bureau des Publications de l'OCDE
2 rue André-Pascal, 75775 PARIS CEDEX 16.
☎ 524.81.67
Principaux correspondants :
13602 AIX-EN-PROVENCE : Librairie de l'Université. ☎ 26.18.08
38000 GRENOBLE : B. Arthaud. ☎ 87.25.11
31000 TOULOUSE : Privat. ☎ 21.09.26
GERMANY – ALLEMAGNE
Verlag Weltarchiv G.m.b.H.
D 2000 HAMBURG 36, Neuer Jungfernstieg 21
☎ 040-35-62-500
GREECE – GRECE
Librairie Kauffmann, 28 rue du Stade,
ATHENES 132. ☎ 322.21.60
HONG-KONG
Government Information Services,
Sales of Publications Office,
1A Garden Road,
☎ H-252281-4
ICELAND – ISLANDE
Snaebjörn Jónsson and Co., h.f.,
Hafnarstræti 4 and 9, P.O.B. 1131,
REYKJAVIK. ☎ 13133/14281/11936
INDIA – INDE
Oxford Book and Stationery Co. :
NEW DELHI, Scindia House. ☎ 47388
CALCUTTA, 17 Park Street. ☎ 24083
IRELAND – IRLANDE
Eason and Son, 40 Lower O'Connell Street,
P.O.B. 42, DUBLIN 1. ☎ 74 39 35
ISRAEL
Emanuel Brown :
35 Allenby Road, TEL AVIV. ☎ 51049/54082
also at :
9, Shlomzion Hamalka Street, JERUSALEM.
☎ 234807
48 Nahlath Benjamin Street, TEL AVIV.
☎ 53276
ITALY – ITALIE
Libreria Commissionaria Sansoni :
Via Lamarmora 45, 50121 FIRENZE. ☎ 579751
Via Bartolini 29, 20155 MILANO. ☎ 365083
Sous-dépositaires :
Editrice e Libreria Herder,
Piazza Montecitorio 120, 00186 ROMA.
☎ 674628
Libreria Hoepli, Via Hoepli 5, 20121 MILANO.
☎ 865446
Libreria Lattes, Via Garibaldi 3, 10122 TORINO.
☎ 519274
La diffusione delle edizioni OCDE è inoltre assicurata dalle migliori librerie nelle città più importanti.

JAPAN – JAPON
OECD Publications Centre,
Akasaka Park Building,
2-3-4 Akasaka,
Minato-ku
TOKYO 107. ☎ 586-2016
Maruzen Company Ltd.,
6 Tori-Nichome Nihonbashi, TOKYO 103,
P.O.B. 5050, Tokyo International 100-31.
☎ 272-7211
LEBANON – LIBAN
Documenta Scientifica/Redico
Edison Building, Bliss Street,
P.O.Box 5641, BEIRUT. ☎ 354429 – 344425
THE NETHERLANDS – PAYS-BAS
W.P. Van Stockum
Buitenhof 36, DEN HAAG. ☎ 070-65.68.08
NEW ZEALAND – NOUVELLE-ZELANDE
The Publications Manager
Government Printing Office
Mulgrave Street (Private Bag)
WELLINGTON, ☎ 737-320
and Government Bookshops at
AUCKLAND (P.O.B. 5344). ☎ 32.919
CHRISTCHURCH (P.O.B. 1721). ☎ 50.331
HAMILTON (P.O.B. 857). ☎ 80.103
DUNEDIN (P.O.B. 1104). ☎ 78.294
NORWAY – NORVEGE
Johan Grundt Tanums Bokhandel,
Karl Johansgate 41/43, OSLO 1. ☎ 02-332980
PAKISTAN
Mirza Book Agency, 65 Shahrah Quaid-E-Azam,
LAHORE 3. ☎ 66839
PHILIPPINES
R.M. Garcia Publishing House,
903 Quezon Blvd. Ext., QUEZON CITY,
P.O. Box 1860 – MANILA. ☎ 99.98.47
PORTUGAL
Livraria Portugal,
Rua do Carmo 70-74. LISBOA 2. ☎ 360582/3
SPAIN – ESPAGNE
Libreria Mundi Prensa
Castello 37, MADRID-1. ☎ 275.46.55
Libreria Bastinos
Pelayo, 52, BARCELONA 1. ☎ 222.06.00
SWEDEN – SUEDE
Fritzes Kungl. Hovbokhandel,
Fredsgatan 2, 11152 STOCKHOLM 16.
☎ 08/23 89 00
SWITZERLAND – SUISSE
Librairie Payot, 6 rue Grenus, 1211 GENEVE 11.
☎ 022-31.89.50
TAIWAN
Books and Scientific Supplies Services, Ltd.
P.O.B. 83, TAIPEI.
TURKEY – TURQUIE
Librairie Hachette,
469 Istiklal Caddesi,
Beyoglu, ISTANBUL, ☎ 44.94.70
et 14 E Ziya Gökalp Caddesi
ANKARA. ☎ 12.10.80
UNITED KINGDOM – ROYAUME-UNI
H.M. Stationery Office, P.O.B. 569, LONDON
SE1 9 NH, ☎ 01-928-6977, Ext. 410
or
49 High Holborn
LONDON WC1V 6HB (personal callers)
Branches at: EDINBURGH, BIRMINGHAM,
BRISTOL, MANCHESTER, CARDIFF,
BELFAST.
UNITED STATES OF AMERICA
OECD Publications Center, Suite 1207,
1750 Pennsylvania Ave, N.W.
WASHINGTON, D.C. 20006. ☎ (202)298-8755
VENEZUELA
Libreria del Este, Avda. F. Miranda 52,
Edificio Galipán, Aptdo. 60 337, CARACAS 106.
☎ 32 23 01/33 26 04/33 24 73
YUGOSLAVIA – YOUGOSLAVIE
Jugoslovenska Knjiga, Terazije 27, P.O.B. 36,
BEOGRAD. ☎ 621-992

Les commandes provenant de pays où l'OCDE n'a pas encore désigné de dépositaire
peuvent être adressées à :
OCDE, Bureau des Publications, 2 rue André-Pascal, 75775 Paris CEDEX 16
Orders and inquiries from countries where sales agents have not yet been appointed may be sent to
OECD, Publications Office, 2 rue André-Pascal, 75775 Paris CEDEX 16

OECD PUBLICATIONS, 2, rue André-Pascal, 75775 Paris Cedex 16 - No. 35.981 1976
PRINTED IN FRANCE